Praise for Have

"A delightful tapestry of stories and experiences from a mother-daughter team who bring a unique perspective to each destination. Their passion and heartfelt narratives from Antarctica to Zululand are a must-have whether you are a world traveler or an armchair adventurer."

– Senator Darryl Rouson—Florida State Senator, Attorney, Upcoming Author

"Heartwarming and inspiring, this book captures the essence of travel through the shared adventure of a mother and daughter, who have traveled to 88 countries, 50 states, and 7 continents. Their stories are both charming and insightful, making this an essential read whether a go-go adventurer or armchair traveler."

– Dr. John Smith—University administrator and professor, author, speaker

"*Have a Love Affair with Travel* is an absolute must-read for anyone with a thirst for adventure and a curiosity for the world. This book isn't just a collection of interesting and fun travel stories; it's a gateway to a life filled with excitement, personal growth, and cultural enrichment. Evelyn and Natalie Kelly's remarkable experiences across seven continents, eighty-eight countries and fifty states, provide inspiration, invaluable lessons, savvy travel hacks that will elevate your travel game and ignite your sense of adventure. Imagine embarking on a journey that will create cherished memories and leave a lasting impact with your loved ones! Cultivate a lifelong love for travel through the guidance of two incredible women who have truly seen it all."

– Malia Rogers, Founder of MediGap Pros, Author & Speaker

"Been There ~ Done That! A phrase that captures the true thrill of travel as you experience the beauty, mystery, and cultures from over 80 countries through the eyes of the authors. You'll be ready to pack your bags for the next adventure as you follow their stories and smart tips across the globe!"

– April Powell, World Traveler, Influencer

Have a Love Affair with TRAVEL

Have a Love Affair with TRAVEL

Your Ticket to an Exhilarating Life

Evelyn Kelly Ph.D. and
Natalie Kelly M.S.

Copyright © 2024 by Evelyn Kelly Ph.D. and Natalie Kelly M.S.

All rights reserved. No part of this publication may be reproduced, stored, or transmitted in any form or by any means without written permission of the publisher or author, except in the case of brief quotations embodied in critical articles and reviews.

Published by travelersatheartLLC

ISBN (paperback): 979-8-9917211-0-3
ISBN (ebook): 979-8-9917211-1-0

Book design and production by www.AuthorSuccess.com
Front cover by www.adobestock.com

Printed in the United States of America

To Charles L. Kelly (1929-2020)
Husband and Dad

Who told us to "Go! Travel!
I will stay home and care for the dogs."

Contents

Introduction ... 1

Part 1: Love of Adventure ... 5

ANTARCTICA: The Penguins' Playground ... 7
CANADA: The Klondike—Not Just an Ice Cream Bar ... 10
ROMANIA: Behind Dracula's Castle Walls ... 12
NEPAL: Close Encounters of a Mountain Kind ... 14
VIETNAM and CAMBODIA: Always Forward, Never Back ... 16
AUSTRALIA: Is the Great Barrier Reef Great? ... 20
AUSTRALIA: Up, Up, and Away in a Hot Air Balloon ... 22
BOLIVIA: A Salty World ... 25
THAILAND: Land of Smiles ... 27
SOUTH AFRICA: Recipe for a Successful Safari ... 30
NEW ZEALAND: Shine Little Glowworm ... 32
CANADA: Banff, Ice Fields, and a $20 Cup of Chili ... 34
TUNISIA: The Arab Spring—We Are There ... 37
IRELAND: I Give You No Blarney ... 40
BRAZIL: Fishing for Piranha ... 43
SAUDI ARABIA: The Mysterious Man ... 46

Part 2: Love of Cultural Enrichment ... 49

CHINA: Traditional Chinese Medicine ... 51
FRANCE: Is Mona Lisa Still Smiling? ... 54
CANADA: Calgary Stampede and Head-Smashed-In Buffalo Jump ... 56
MOROCCO: The Little Sales Boy ... 59
ICELAND: Trip to the Moon ... 61
COSTA RICA: Fruit Bowl of the World ... 64
ECUADOR: Standing on Two Sides of the Equator ... 67
EL SALVADOR: Walk a Mile in their Shoes ... 69
COLOMBIA: Thumbs Up to Colombia ... 71
GUATEMALA: Land of Eternal Spring ... 74
ARUBA, BONAIRE, AND CURACAO: ... 77
A-B-Cs of the Southern Caribbean
NORWAY: Land of Firsts ... 80
USA: The Long Grey Line—Tales from West Point ... 83

EGYPT: More than Pyramids	86
HUNGARY: Eternal Vigilance is the Price of Freedom	89

Part 3: Love of Personal Growth and Building Relationships — 93

BOLIVIA: Two Worlds	95
PERU: Machu Picchu—Where the Happy Overcomes the Miserable	98
RUSSIA: Peasants' Road to Moscow	101
SOUTH AFRICA: Where the Compass Needles Go Haywire	104
FRANCE: Under the Eiffel Tower	106
FRANCE: In Love and War	108
FRANCE: We're Not in Kansas Anymore	111
INDIA: Culture Shock and the Land of Extremes	114
AUSTRIA, USA, Michigan: A Tale of Two Chapels "Silent Night"	117
LITHUANIA: Hill of Crosses—Was It the Devil Who Made Me Do It?	119
DENMARK: Hans Christian Andersen and The Ugly Duckling	122
INDIA: Taj Mahal—A True Love Story	125
JAPAN: From Okinawa with Love	128
GUAM: Exotic Surprise and the Simple Life	132
ISRAEL: No Worries; It's Okay	135

Part 4: Love for Nature, Environment, and the Animal World — 139

ECUADOR: Movie Stars of the Galapagos	141
USA, ALASKA: Calling the Wild	143
ALASKA, U.S: Man's Best Friend	147
SCOTLAND, USA., SOUTH AFRICA: Dedicated Dogs	150
ROMANIA: The Dogs of Bucharest	153
USA: Blue Dog	155
GREECE: Cats of the Acropolis	157
USA, GREECE, RUSSIA: For the Love of Horses	159
BULGARIA: The Dancing Bears	162
BRAZIL: The Amazon Experience	164
NICARAGUA: Land of Volcanoes, Lakes, and Castrated Raccoons	167
FRANCE: Claude Monet—From Class Clown to Nature Lover	169
TUNISIA: Humps, Lumps, and BMWs	171

Part 5: Love for Education and Lifelong Learning — 175

EGYPT: Mummy and Daughter in Search of Imhotep	177
MEXICO: The Day of the Dead	180

MEXICO: Dreaming Through Their Eyes—Frida and Diego	183
FRANCE: Van Gogh—Yellow House and Sunflowers	186
EASTER ISLAND: Beyond the Moai Statues	188
USA: Life on the Lower Mississippi	191
PANAMA: More Than a Canal	195
CUBA: A Land Frozen in Time	198

Part 6: Love for Fun, Food, Festivities — 201

Our Love Affair with Toilets of the World	203
USA—Upper Mississippi: IS Mark Twain Still Alive?	206
SOUTH AFRICA: Dancing with the Zulus	209
SOUTH AFRICA: Standing on Ostrich Eggs	211
AUSTRALIA: Rugby, Futbol, and American Football	214
USA: On the Trail with Lewis and Clark	216
USA: Sleepy Hollow Is Not So Sleepy	220
SAINT VINCENT: Goat Head Soup, Birthday Party in Saint Vincent	222
BRAZIL: Boat Full of Santas	224
UNITED ARAB EMIRATES: Snow Boarding in Dubai	227
GERMANY: Eating a Hamburger in Hamburg and a Frankfurter in Frankfurt: Surviving Europe on a Budget	230
USA, KEY WEST: A Great Place to Be a Rooster	233

Part 7: Cheers to Travel: Smooth Trips, Smart Tips, and Fun Tricks — 237

From Wish to Bliss	239
Conclusion	264
Acknowledgments	265

Introduction

Natalie and I have finally fulfilled our out-of-reach dream of going to Paris. As I entered our hotel room and opened the bathroom door, I saw something unusual—two toilets. Why two toilets? What is the use of a second toilet? We had a mystery on our hands the mystery of the two toilets.

Our traveling companions were just as baffled. One woman said she washed clothes in it; a college student said he thought it was for washing hair. One ingenious couple put ice in the bowl to chill wine. When we arrived home, we found the answer to our puzzle.

So why did this mother and daughter leave their comfort zones and enter an unknown world with such mysteries as two toilets?

It all started in 1992, when I ran for political office. After several months of grueling campaigning, election night came. I lost by a few votes!

Out of the blue, my husband Charles said, "Why don't you and Natalie go to Europe? You both have worked hard on this campaign and deserve a break."

When I proposed the trip to Natalie, she loved the idea BUT had some concerns. Natalie had her own reality show. She was the youngest female staff director in the male-dominated world of the Florida Senate. Could she get off work for several weeks? Could she afford the cost? **And** who was going to take care of her dog?

Charles answered all our questions. "Just GO!" he said. "I will care for the dogs."

So, in July of 1993, Natalie and I took off for Europe and never were there any greener, more naive, and inexperienced travelers than we. Our trip was booked for three weeks to visit thirteen countries. As for relaxation, it was getting up at 5:00 a.m. with bags out and ready to go. We had a different hotel almost every night. At the end of the road in Athens, we said, "Okay, there is the Acropolis; let's go home."

Nevertheless, on our way home, we both agreed, "That was fun. Where do we want to go next year?"

The travel bug bit us. We were hooked.

So here we are, many moons from 1993, having traveled to seven continents, eighty-eight countries (and counting), and fifty states. It has been a fantastic journey. We cannot tell you what travel has meant to us, but in this book, we want to convey how travel has enriched our lives and can do the same for you.

This book is a collection of seventy-nine stories in six parts. At the end of each story, we suggest a SMART TIP—a lesson or advice about the specific country. However, this book is more than a collection of adventures; it is a resource for managing the complexities of travel. The seventh part offers a guide to smooth trips, smart tips, and fun tricks.

We show the difference between tourists and travelers: a tourist wants to escape life, looking for the comforts and conveniences of home. A traveler wants to experience life and seeks to understand the culture and adapt. This book will help you be that SMART traveler, not just a casual tourist. Travel is your ticket to an exhilarating life.

What's in it For You

- By the time you have finished this book, you will appreciate how travel can enrich:
- Your expectation of adventure
- Your understanding of other cultures
- Your personal growth and social connections
- Your appreciation of nature and the animal world
- Your desire for lifelong learning
- Your fun, food, and festivities
- Your becoming a master globetrotter

Cheers to your travel,

Evelyn and Natalie Kelly

PART 1

Love of Adventure

This is for adventure seekers who like hiking, scuba diving, fishing, and hot air ballooning.

Also, for those who like to go to unusual, exotic places.

Adventure can include exploring diverse landscapes, from mountains to beaches to jungles. Traveling to these places can be incredibly exciting and fulfilling—especially afterward when you tell about it.

ANTARCTICA:
The Penguins' Playground

The film *March of the Penguins* inspired two Floridians to become interested in Antarctica's continent and see those resilient birds in black tuxedos. How can such creatures survive and thrive under harsh conditions? They have wings, but they cannot fly. They are birds that act like fish.

Natalie and I board a Norwegian icebreaker to visit "The White Continent" and the penguins' playground. The staff provides bright blue parkas with all the appropriate bells and whistles for our excursions off the ship. We are given special boots to slosh through an antiseptic solution every time we step on and off the continent. As we climb onto unique rubber rafts and head for Half Moon Island, we have strict orders not to touch or chase penguins.

Wow! Here, we trek the cobbled beaches that are inhabited by a colony of penguins with streaks of black feathers running from ear to ear. They are called "chin straps." It is December 11, near the beginning of summer, and the colony is in a flurry of activity. We march along with one group as they waddle to the beach. Heads up in the air, they ignore us but move in a zombie-like line. As their torpedo-shaped bodies sail into the water, they look like graceful ballerinas, dancing, twisting, and jumping. This chowtime "dance" would fill their bellies with fish, squid, and krill, a shrimp lookalike.

We climb back into the rubber raft, go through the disinfectant, and observe the magnificent scenery until the next excursion. We see something unusual— blue ice. It is everywhere. In contrast to its "white continent" nickname, Antarctica is every shade of blue. This ice occurs when snow falls on a glacier, is compressed, and becomes part of the glacier. Air bubbles are squeezed out, and the enlarged ice crystals make the ice's color blue.

Later, we will see two more of the eighteen other kinds of penguins: the Gentoos and Adelies.

Adelies Thought We Were Big, Ugly Penguins

Ready to go again. We are at the location of a massive colony of Adelie penguins, which you most associate with penguins in advertisements. They are plain black and white with pudgy pink feet. After their swim, the thirty-nine-degree water of summer causes a heat wave. To cool off, the birds pump their flippers like they are waving their arms. With small, thin feathers on the underside of their flippers, their body heat escapes. These penguins dive deep and can remain underwater for five minutes or more.

We move to a rocky crag to observe the organized chaos of the colony. Natalie suggests that instead of watching the entire colony, we watch a small area of birds in action.

Penguins behave like people. Some are busily gathering stones to make the nest for their brood that will come a month later. One old

Three Gentoo penguins we name Larry, Curly, and Moe waddle their way to the waves, soaking up the applause from their adoring fans

grouch sits down to relax, snap, and grumble at any other bird passing by. A few hooligans steal the stones from the workers' nests when they are not looking. Others are just standing doing nothing. Penguins have counterparts in human society.

Observing the Gentoos

Our next colony is the Gentoos. Gentoos look like they are wearing a white bonnet and have a bright red-orange bill. We note something unique: they distance and arrange themselves in an almost grid-like pattern. This may be to keep out of each other's pecking or slapping range.

The penguins' playground contains unknowns, surprises, and terrific memories. Best of all, we have encountered marvelous creatures whose lives are as complex and complicated as ours.

SMART TIP: If you want to visit Antarctica, choose a trip that offers on-land excursions. However, minimizing the human impact on this pristine environment is crucial. Always follow guidelines set by tour operators, such as using disinfectants to prevent introducing foreign pathogens. Observe wildlife from a respectful distance. Remember, while the penguins' habitat offers incredible photo opportunities, we must preserve their home by leaving it as untouched as possible.

CANADA: The Klondike— Not Just an Ice Cream Bar

Dawson City, Yukon, a place frozen not only by the weather but also in time. The streets are not paved; wooden sidewalks lead us around town. This town reminds us of old Western movies.

Stampeding for Gold

In the Klondike Valley, Dawson City became the center of the famous Gold Rush (1896-1899). Overnight, the town evolved from a small First Nations camp to a thriving city of 17,000. When the gold ran out, the population plummeted.

On August 16, 1896, three sourdoughs (Klondike residents) found gold in Rabbit (Bonanza) Creek. A huge timber structure with pictures of the three adventurers marks the discovery claim site. We walk down a small incline to the edge of the fast-running Bonanza Creek; we do not find gold nuggets today.

Now is our time to join the thousands of Stampeders who came to this land to moil for gold. At the Dawson City Museum, we spy pictures that make our blood run cold. Two queues of men are climbing snow-covered summits to get to Dawson City. The rigorous trails became animal killers and were even deadlier for men who died of murders, suicides, disease, malnutrition, hypothermia, and avalanches.

Dawson City was as wild as the mountains surrounding it. We are reminded of this when we go to Diamond Tooth Gertie's for a can-can show and gambling afterward. We skip the gambling to eat poutine: a native sourdough dish of French fries loaded with cheese and smothered with gravy. It is a hearty meal, but not for those looking at the scales.

The Sour Toe Cocktail

On our second night, we go to the Downtown Hotel for the rite of passage for visitors to Dawson City: the Sour Toe Cocktail. People line up for a shot of whiskey with a fermented human toe inside the glass. You get a club membership certificate if you are strong enough to carry it through. Natalie was number 104,373. Her certificate reads, "You can drink it fast; you can drink it slow, but your lips must touch the toe." Legend has it that the original toe belonged to a bootlegger who preserved his frostbitten toe in moonshine. In 1973, a Yukon riverboat captain found the toe in an abandoned cabin, and the Sour Toe Cocktail was born.

We leave our city "on top of the world" with great interest in human motivation. Why would people leave their homes to wander in this great white unknown? The rush to Dawson ended as quickly as it began when gold was found in Nome, Alaska. A few men did get rich; most did not. However, the storekeepers, saloon keepers, gamblers, and prostitutes made a good living.

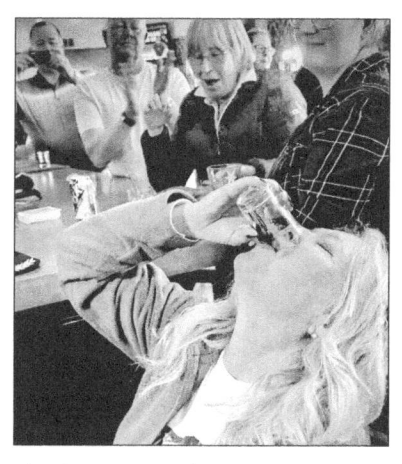

The Sour Toe Cocktail is a unique and shocking tradition of the quirky spirit of Dawson City. Natalie downs the Sour Toe Cocktail quickly as she touches the fermented toe with her lip.

SMART TIP: Whether panning for gold or participating in local customs like the Sour Toe Cocktail, do so with an awareness of the area's heritage and support businesses that invest in preserving the local history and environment.

ROMANIA:
Behind Dracula's Castle Walls

Bran is a castle, a mansion, a home, a place of horror, and the setting of Bram Stoker's novel *Dracula*. It is also the main destination in Transylvania, a historical area in Central Romania.

Our guide, Sophia, sets the atmosphere as we traverse the dark Carpathian Mountains, where dense spruce forests are the home of brown bears, wolves, and folklore. We see the white mists rising from the forest; supposedly spirits that come out to dance and play. "If they seduce you, you may disappear forever without a trace," she warns.

Perched precariously on a high rock is the massive Bran Castle, which looks like a huge blob of light caramel. The thick limestone fortress walls are pock-marked from many battles and capped by round towers called donjons. We are breathless. It is as excellent as the first site of the Acropolis, Red Square in Moscow, or the Egyptian pyramids.

Bran Castle is a dramatic image perched on a high rock and surrounded by the mysterious Carpathian Mountains, where Dracula's legend adds a spine-chilling mystery.

CLIMBING ONE HUNDRED STEPS

To get to the first floor, we climb one hundred steps. To move up to the top, we navigate a secret passage that is so narrow and twisting that it is wide enough for only one person. Pulling ourselves up with a sturdy rope connected to both sides is no simple feat. We reach a lookout that enables us to see miles of the surrounding country. We imagine we are pouring hot oil down on the enemy through the large openings in the walls.

Have a passion for the morbid and grotesque? There is the Iron Maiden, a solid iron cabinet with a hinged door fitted with spikes inside, and the Cradle of Judah, a pyramid-like chair designed for tremendous pain. Displayed are all kinds of tools of barbarism with an explanation of how they worked.

Transylvania folklore existed long before Bram Stoker spawned tales of Dracula. Bloodsucking creatures called "Strigoi" roamed the shadowy halls. However, Stoker modeled his predator after a real-life person: Vlad III, son of Dracul, prince of Wallachia. He is also known as Vlad the Impaler and Vlad Tapes. At the same time, we may think of him as a monster and vampire. During his time, he was a mighty hero who fought to protect the area against the invaders from the Ottoman Empire. And yes, he did impale enemies, positioning them along the roads to show what would happen to you if you dared to attack. (He learned the technique when imprisoned by the Ottoman Turks).

On our return, Sophia asked, "So, do you think it was Dracula's castle? It's up to you to decide."

We pondered the question as we returned to Bucharest that night and ate in the Count Dracula Restaurant. Lining the walls was a long display of pictures of guess who? Vlad Tepes, their hero.

SMART TIP: Getting to Bran Castle is not easy. Consider an excursion from Bucharest, Romania, with a local tour company or a knowledgeable local guide who can offer historical insights and contextualize folklore.

NEPAL: Close Encounters of a Mountain Kind

The crowded marketplace is alive with wafting smells from rich Asian spices, incense, and vehicle exhaust. We watch the people as they push the massive bells for prayer. We are in Kathmandu, the mysterious capital of Nepal.

Watching the Healer

Our guide, Kumar, tells us we are in luck. The healer is here today, and we join to watch. A long line of people with different infirmities is crowded around an area with numerous bed-like concrete slabs. The healer or doctor, the Dhami Jhankrior, is dressed in a long overcoat with huge laden pockets.

According to Kumar, the young man we are observing has terrible headaches. The healer passes something over the young man's head as he reclines on one of the concrete slabs. As he closes his eyes, the healer prays for him and calls out evil spirits. He snaps his fingers, and the man jumps up and sees a great light. He pays the healer, who is getting ready for his next patient, a man with a wooden stick.

Over the Himalayas

We must move on to our next adventure at 6:00 the next morning—to the Himalayas from the skies. A super early rise is essential for the hour-long ride. We approach a small plane. Buddha Air is emblazoned across the side. Everyone is guaranteed a window because only one seat is on each side of the aisle.

If one could ever wish for a close encounter of a mountain kind, this is it. Nepal contains most of the highest mountain ranges and shares eight of the world's ten highest peaks. Taking off from the Kathmandu airport, which has the most rigorous security, we hold our breath at the sound of the loud motor. As we approach the mountains, we follow majestic ranges up and down. We fly between sparkling peaks—yes, we can almost touch them. Mountains create unforgiving winds. Is it our imagination that we were suddenly pushed upward? Flying between these mountains is quite scary.

We then emerge to glimpse at lakes and glaciers with clear water flowing down. And suddenly, the massive Mount Everest is in front of us—breathtaking. We are above the clouds. Viewing the mountains from on top of the world is a sobering experience.

How humbling—we have experienced an exercise in perspective, capable of making two tiny humans feel much smaller and even less significant.

The hour passes rapidly, but not soon enough. The engine sounds like it is skipping. I think Natalie is praying. It works, and the plane lands safely.

This was quite an encounter of a mountain kind. To remind us, we were given a t-shirt that reads, "I flew over the Himalayas on Buddha Air."

The close encounter with the Himalayas was a unique and thrilling experience. Soaring with Buddha Air, there it was: the jaw-dropping majesty of Mount Everest.

SMART TIP: For those who prefer soaring over peaks to scaling them, a flight over the Himalayas offers a thrilling alternative to mountain trekking. Take a sky-high adventure—it's all about finding your summit experience.

VIETNAM and CAMBODIA: Always Forward, Never Back

Over a hundred scooters are coming right at us as we try to cross the street in Ho Chi Minh City. We panic and jump back onto the sidewalk. How do you cross the road? Where is the crosswalk? Certainly, the joke "Why did the chicken cross the road?" did not make it to Vietnam. The chicken never would have made it to the other side.

Scooters and tuk-tuks (mini truck taxis) are kings in Vietnam and Cambodia. The streets appear like a gaggle of geese running in all directions, honking and beeping.

Our guide, Duc, is beside us. "Go ahead," he says.

What? No way. Duc smiles calmly, sticks his hand into the traffic, and slowly walks across the bustling street as scooters buzz around us. We make it without a hit, bump, or even a scratch.

Evelyn asks, "How did you do that?"

He says, "There is a trick to Vietnamese traffic: always look forward, never back."

Look forward, never back seems to be the motto of these two countries.

Never Back

As we leave our hotel in Hanoi, a happy young man is at the desk. He has a different haircut—a mixture of the long-haired crew cut. I comment on it, and he says in perfect English, "I am the new generation of Vietnamese."

We see this new generation as a beacon of progress, immaculate and service-oriented, filled with friendly, helpful, and smiling people, instilling a sense of reassurance and confidence in our travel plans.

Nice Surprises in Cambodia

While we are walking up to the Royal Palace in Phnom Penh, the king drives by in his motorcade. Cambodia has a constitutional monarchy, but the Cambodian People's Party, formed under communist ideology, leads the government.

We spend an entire day exploring Cambodia's temples. The architectural masterpieces of Angkor Thom and Angkor Wat are UNESCO World Heritage Sites. Built during the twelfth century, Angkor Wat's five towers rise through three levels to a grand central shrine. A wide moat surrounds it, representing the outer edge of the universe. Every part is full of history and meaning to Hindu and Buddhist traditions.

We stop at a fast food place on the side of the road, which our guide called "KFC" or Kambodian Fried Crickets. We are offered a selection of fried silk cocoons, huge water roaches, crickets, or frogs. Evelyn chooses fried crickets, which taste like chicken.

Reason Not to Look Back

Back in the city, the prison museum is a reminder to "never look back." The ruthless dictator Pol Pot inflicted atrocities and horrors on the people during the reign of the Khmer Rouge from 1975 to 1979. He used forced labor, resettlements, torture, and starvation of those who were intellectuals or who opposed the utopian vision of a classless agrarian society. A war with Vietnam finally ended these killing fields and helped restore reason in 1992.

Evelyn meets one of the survivors of the killing fields. Our guide expressed how this negatively impacted families. After we inquire about the plight of the people, he breaks down. We cry with him. He tells us of his mother and dad, who were rounded up with a group of young people. They were forced to get married, although they did not know each other, and the guards watched to see if they consummated the marriage. They were tortured and forced to work on farms seven days a week for twelve hours a day.

Vietnam

Vietnam's beauty is astounding. We see temples, shops, picturesque countryside, endless rice paddies, and a fascinating world, from the French-style architecture of Hoi An to the cruise along the Mekong Delta River.

We do an optional half-day tour of the Cu Chi tunnels of the Viet Cong. These 125 miles of tunnels were amazing for connecting underground hideouts, weapons, and hospitals, and even passing under US headquarters. Natalie decides to descend into one of the tunnels just as the American soldiers, called tunnel rats by the Vietnamese, did when they discovered them.

The Dragon Bridge in Da Nang isn't just stunning—it's a dragon-shaped marvel that roars to life with fiery breath at night.

Our Perspective

We have mixed emotions about this unusual adventure. We realize these were charming places with fascinating history and people, but we also realize it is an area that had been troubled. Travel makes us fall in love with these two countries; on the other hand, we realize the sacrifices of lives and limbs made by both sides.

SMART TIP: Nevertheless, in the spirit of adventure, we found what travel can do for people. It has changed our lives to look forward, never back.

AUSTRALIA:
Is the Great Barrier Reef Great?

By Natalie

We fly from Melbourne to Cairns, Queensland, home to the Great Barrier Reef and a tropical rainforest. This city is pronounced like "cans," and they will correct you if you call it anything else.

Scuba Diving at the Great Barrier Reef

We take a ship to a platform built on the reef's edge. The crystal clear water reveals intricate details of the coral gardens and the diverse species that call the reef home.

I decide to take more of an adventurer's visit. I am going to scuba dive for the FIRST TIME. What better place to learn to dive than on the Great Barrier Reef? How hard can it be, given I am a very good swimmer?

They showed us a film on scuba diving, so I signed my life away and donned the rubber suit. They help us with our tanks and show us how to breathe. Sure, I can do this. We will be hoisted down in a metal cage with the top open. There will be three levels, with the third the deepest.

The immersion begins. As I descend into the depths, I encounter schools of colorful fish and, even more majestic, a small shark below me. The surreal beauty of the corals, the sensation of weightlessness, and the silence of the underwater world provide a profound connection with nature. I am not frightened as we began sinking.

The cage stops; we are at the first level platform. And then it hits me, and I panic. I cannot breathe! I know I am going to die. My only thought is to get out, and because the top is open, I spring out of the cage and shoot to the surface. I am thoroughly vilified and castigated—and told how dangerous it is to come out and ascend so quickly. I could get the bends. But the bends sound like a better choice than dying in the depths. After I get back to the platform, I am okay. My panic attack is over, and I can breathe again.

Adventure on the Skyrail Rainforest Cableway

The next day, we are scheduled for a cable car ride over the tropical rainforest. Although we are up in the air, this ride gives me a unique perspective of one of the oldest tropical forests. Like in Canada, the indigenous people are called the First Nations. We also attend a show performed by native dancers. I must have "sucker" written on my forehead, because I am always pulled out to dance. I even get to play a unique instrument called a didgeridoo—a long cylindrical tube developed over 1,000 years ago that sounds like a sick, bellowing cow.

Since coming home from Australia, I have never had a panic attack again.

SMART TIP: If you're planning adventurous activities like scuba diving at the Great Barrier Reef, preparing adequately before your trip is crucial. Participate in pre-trip training sessions or complete a certified course, especially if you are a beginner. This preparation helps ensure you are comfortable and safe, reducing the risk of panic or injury.

AUSTRALIA: Up, Up, and Away in a Hot Air Balloon

After spending the night in Cairns (pronounced Cans), we are ready for more Aussie fun, this time in a hot air balloon. We are awakened at 5:00 a.m. to make the journey inland by bus. We will be flying over the Outback, an area that is remote from everywhere.

We ride on the bus and then empty into a large field of short grass. Sitting in a clearing is a vast straw-colored basket with a rim about six feet off the ground. The basket is tied to the ground by ropes and secured by spikes. Our balloon has a huge yellow and blue world map. This is the Tropical North Queensland Hot Air Balloon.

Up, Up, and Away

The height of the basket is a challenge to climb, but we are helped (pushed) into the basket. As we wait, we look up, and above us are various gadgets with gauges. Four round cylinders generate hot air to fill the balloon. We are experiencing a basic scientific principle: warmer air rises in cooler air, so these are the instruments of heating the air to get us to rise. We are happy that the operator knows which gauges to turn. So, with lots of whooshing, swishing, and yelling to guys on the ground to unhook the ropes, we are off and gently rising straight up. Once we reach a certain altitude, we drift quietly.

Below is a wealth of jaw-dropping beauty. We look over and see towns—Cairns and Port Douglas. The grass looks autumn-brown but has some trees of color. Other balloons are in the air. One balloon has red and white stripes; another balloon is yellow with a red top.

As we float forward, we can locate parts of the rainforest. We see the Daintree River and will soon ride in a boat to hear songs like "Waltzing Matilda" and "Tie Me Kangaroo Down, Mate."

Kangaroos are everywhere in the wild. They hop as if trying to keep up with us, but they are more like running away.

We are flying in the clouds. Natalie confesses that, although she fears heights, she has absolutely none of that in this basket. We feel very secure.

We are again shooshing as he begins the descent. We glide down very softly. Guys grab the ropes to keep the balloon steady as we land. The operator asks if we would help him fold the balloon, and we follow his directions.

Animal Farm

What would a visit to Australia be without seeing its unusual animals? We had seen kangaroos in the wild, and back in Sydney, we will see more of them at the Featherdale Wildlife Park. This park is eight acres long, provides animal enclosures and visitor facilities, and specializes in Australian wildlife and birds. We are able to pet joeys (young kangaroos) and wallabies, a cousin of the kangaroo.

One star we do not see is the white dingo. The dingo looks like a dog—or is it a wolf? Some say it is neither, but an early offshoot of all modern dog breeds, between the wolf and domesticated dogs.

One of our favorites is the Tasmanian devil, which looks like a small dog. They are very stocky and black with white markings. This marsupial has strong jaws and claws and is mainly a scavenger. It crushes and eats bones and fur, creating a lot of crunchy-sounding noise when eating.

We enjoyed our adventure to Australia and meeting its energetic blokes and sheilas.

SMART TIP: Australians are friendly, open, and relaxed. But, if you use the thumbs-up hand sign to an Australian, they may not take it well. It is a derogatory hand gesture.

BOLIVIA:
A Salty World

Our guide picks us up in Potosi, Bolivia, to take us through the Great Salt Flats. After driving for about five hours, we first see a salt desert. How spectacular it is! The desert had been a lake that dried up and left huge white hexagonal plates of salt as far as you could see.

As our jeep crunches along on the salt with no roads or signs, we comprehend the meaning of infinity. All perspective is turned upside down. Clouds above reflect on the ground; we are floating among the clouds. We see a few brave souls out in the middle of the flats exhibiting silly poses. Our driver tells us to do the same. He walks onto the salt flat and makes a funny pose. Our guide asks Natalie to hold her hand out while she takes a picture. Here Natalie is holding up our 160 pound driver with one hand.

The Great Salt Flats of Bolivia are one of the most surreal places in the world. Like Natalie and her guide, visitors have fun posing to create whimsical illusions.

A Salt Motel

After miles and miles of travel in the salt desert, our jeep pulls into the world's most remote motel, Tayka del Desierto. This hotel is made of salt. As we traverse the salt floors through a salt lobby to our salt room, we run our hands along the salt walls. In this remote location, solar energy creates a heating system based on radiation that circulates hot water and emits heat. We are told to use the shower before 4:00 p.m. because that is when it shuts off. It becomes very cold.

We are exhausted from our long day of traveling through the salt desert and decide to retire early. There is no television. I jump on the bed; wow—this bed is hard. "Of course it's hard; it's a block of salt," laughs Natalie. We are sleeping on a one-inch cotton mattress on a salt slab.

On the Road Again

We are on the road again after breakfast on a salt table. Natalie says, "I had a terrible dream last night. We were stuck on the salt flats and left to die."

We travel for about an hour, and the car starts smoking. Is Natalie's dream coming true? The local director, Jeanette, assures us that Jose, the driver, is a master mechanic. After five hours, he does manage to fix the car enough to hobble into town to the plane that will take us home.

Of our eighty-eight countries and travels, the salty world was the most memorable. It was the best of trips and the worst of trips.

SMART TIP: Ensure you're seasoned enough before going on an extreme adventure! Exploring the salt desert is like navigating another planet, so it's best to have a few travel experiences before tackling this salty spectacle.

THAILAND: Land of Smiles

By Jonathan Pait
with Natalie and Evelyn

A surprise awaited me before I headed home on leave—I would be spending Christmas in Phuket, Thailand. My friends and I were ready for a week of relaxation, adventure, and exploration in this wild country known as the "Land of Smiles."

Thailand was like nothing I had ever experienced before. When our ship docked at the port, I could feel this country's energy pulsing through my veins. The ride to the mainland was not for the faint of heart. The swells crashed against our ferry, tossing us up and down like rag dolls. I held onto my stomach as we finally reached land, grateful to have made it in one piece.

The Eccentric Character

As we stepped off the ferry, a sea of Thailanders greeted us with loud cheers and frantic arm waving. The colorful tuk-tuks caught our attention, reminding us that we were not in Kansas anymore. I looked around, overwhelmed by the chaos, when suddenly my eyes locked with a man who would soon become our driver for the next four days. He was an eccentric character with wild hair and a mischievous twinkle in his eye. He called out, promising to take us anywhere we wanted for a hundred dollars. Without hesitation, I summoned my travel companions, and we jumped into the beat-up green cab, eager to explore this vibrant country. As we drove through the bustling streets, our driver greeted us with stories about the most popular places in Thailand.

We asked him to take us to the best restaurant on the island; his eyes lit up with excitement. We followed his lead and were soon immersed in a world of mouth-watering, spicy Thai food. I couldn't tell you the exact names of the dishes we tried, but I will never forget the explosion of flavors that danced on my tongue. Our driver became our guide, taking us to places off the beaten path and showing us Thailand's true heart and soul. He took us to a hidden bar decorated with 1920s memorabilia and owned by an Australian man who fulfilled his dream of owning a speakeasy in Thailand.

Hanging with the Tigers

The next day, our driver asked if we wanted to pet tigers. Of course, being adventurous souls, we eagerly agreed. We drove up into the mountains, surrounded by fog and winding roads that felt like something out of Jurassic Park. When we arrived at a tiger rescue facility, we were greeted by a guide who led us into an empty enclosure. A massive tiger appeared before us. Being so close to such a gigantic, majestic creature was surreal. We were allowed to pet and play with the tiger, and I will never forget the feeling of its massive arm on my shoulder. We also got to play with adorable tiger cubs, and I couldn't stop smiling as they jumped and nuzzled against my legs.

As I reflect on my time in Thailand, I can't help but feel grateful for the unexpected adventures and amazing people that I met along the way. It taught me to embrace the unknown and to say yes to new experiences, no matter how out of my comfort zone. Thailand captured my heart, and I know I will always carry a piece of it wherever my travels take me.

SMART TIP: Engage with wildlife through reputable sanctuaries that prioritize animal welfare, and always verify the ethical standards of any unusual activity, such as interacting with tigers or adventure sports.

SOUTH AFRICA:
Recipe for a Successful Safari

Ask Prince William and Kate Middleton, who are dedicated to wildlife, why people are so enthralled with safaris. Their environmental interest is different from that of the legendary hunts of Theodore Roosevelt or Ernest Hemingway, who were interested in finding big games for trophies. The stories of Hemingway, the born adventurer, popularized the word "safari."

Many national parks are available for safaris in Africa: Serengeti National Park, a World Heritage site; the Hwange National Park in Zimbabwe; and the Masai Mara National Reserve in Tanzania. We are on safari in Kruger National Park in South Africa.

One element of a successful safari is seeing the variety of wildlife in the natural environment. A successful one means seeing all the Big Five animals in the wild: lion, leopard, elephant, rhinoceros, and Cape buffalo. These are the so-called "Big Five" because they are the hunters' favorites.

At a South African animal refuge dedicated to healing injured wildlife, Natalie pets the majestic cheetah as part of her unforgettable experience.

In the Safari Jeep

The landscape's natural beauty strikes us as we climb into the jeep. The place looks golden. The hues of the vast expanses of grassland send an aura that make the air alive as the waves of midday heat trickle down. There are scattered islands of trees, such as the acacia. Their flowers bloom at the end of sharp-curved thorns. A lone tree provides a large umbrella-like top, giving animals shelter from the sun.

How lucky we are to see all of the big five. Viewing animal behavior adds to the meaning of the safari. We see animals in the herd and are told about their hunting techniques, mating rituals, etc. As we move on, suddenly, our guide stops the jeep.

"Look behind you," he says.

The leopard, normally a secretive big cat that stays hidden in the scrubby bush, crosses the road behind our jeep. The knowledgeable guide points out animal behavior and sees things the average person would not. We would never have thought to look behind us.

The Cape buffalo looks very placid as he drinks at a water hole, but its huge horns and aggressive temperament make it one of the most ferocious mammals.

We see zebras and wildebeest together like a harmonious family, and rhinos resting under the brush. At the watering hole, hippos and their babies are in the water with giraffes that spread out their front legs to drink from the pond. Hundreds of impalas, the favorite food of big cats, are running away from the sound of the jeep. We have an unusual picture moment when a lion has just killed its prey and is enjoying its feast.

Safaris can be fun, something to cherish in your memory, and something to tell great stories about. We did get to see all the BIG FIVE and had a successful safari.

SMART TIP: Research. You will invest a lot in the safari and the flight to get there. In a search engine, hunt for "best safaris." You will get many suggestions, so ask for their brochures and talk to your travel agent, who is your very best guide.

NEW ZEALAND:
Shine Little Glowworm

By Evelyn

I step gingerly into the small, rickety boat with Natalie and six others. We are in the village of Waitomo, about two hours south of Auckland, New Zealand. We are now descending an underground river into the dark bowels of the earth to the Cave of the Glowworms. We have no idea what to expect.

I remember summer nights in Tennessee when we chased fireflies or lightning bugs and put them in a jar. We watched them twinkle and shine and wondered how they did it. I remember a song with a lilting melody and words that encouraged a glowworm to shine and glimmer.

Light at the End of the Cave

As we descend into the dark depths, church-mouse quiet except for the paddle shoosh-shooshing against the water, it is very cold, and water is dripping from somewhere onto our heads.

"Look up!" I hear.

In blackness, a myriad of stars appear before our eyes! It looks like those that shine and twinkle along the Milky Way. The tiny beings are showing off for us. They are letting their little blue-green lights shine—shine-shine from the limestone roof of the cave.

We paddle on, "oohing" and "aahing." These little cave-top glowworms are not the same as the lightning bugs flitting about on a summer night. They are insects called *Arachnocampa luminous*. They emit their light off and on to attract mates and entice prey, which they capture with sticky threads that hang down from their bodies.

Looking for the Perfect Male Worm

During this hour-long ride, we are entertained by a chemical reaction. Females use the bioluminescent pulsing light to entice the attention of male glowworms to get them to fly up and mate with them. The products of the mating are larvae stuck to the roof, which also glow and attract mosquitoes and other insects into their sticky threads.

How can this light be? The scientific explanation is that the chemical reaction takes place in cells called photocytes. The enzyme luciferase excites a pigment, luciferin, producing the light. This is a similar process to the one we experienced with lightning bugs.

As I emerge from the Cave of the Glowworms, I blink and warm up a little. What an experience! But is there a lesson from the twinkling lights of the cave? I saw small insects living a happy life as nature intended. I relate it to a simple children's song . . . *This little light of mine, I'm gonna let it shine*.

SMART TIP: Remember to respect the natural habitat by following all guidelines, such as not taking photos inside the caves, which could disrupt the glowworms' environment. This responsible approach ensures that these magical creatures continue to thrive.

CANADA: Banff, Ice Fields, and a $20 Cup of Chili

By Natalie

We are excited to be in Banff, Canada, on the most historic day—July 1, 2022—the celebration of Canada's 150th birthday. Banff is indeed quaint. We are staying at the historic King Edward Hotel, built by George Stephen, a pioneer developer of the Canadian Pacific Railway. He named this small village after his hometown of Banff, Scotland.

We enjoy watching performances by First Nations (the Canadian name for Native people), Ukrainian folk dancers, and the Falun Dafa, a group banned in China.

A $20 Cup of Chili

Leaving Banff, we travel along the Trans-Canadian Highway, a scenic highway that runs through the Canadian Rockies and is considered one of the most beautiful drives in the world. Along this stretch of highway, we see stunning views of towering peaks, glaciers, turquoise lakes, and abundant wildlife.

The scenic drive—Banff to Jasper—takes three and a half hours and is spectacular, although it is cold and drizzly. About halfway to our destination, we pull into the Crossing Restaurant. Our guide says, "This is the only place to eat for miles. A buffet is in the back, but it is rather expensive." Mother settles for a cup of chili. When we receive the tab, t is a whopping $20.

Slipping and Sliding

Our last stop on the highway is one night in Jasper before my most memorable adventure—visiting the Columbia Icefield covering a glacier. A special bus called an Ice Explorer takes us to the field. I call it a "moon buggy." It has tires that are as tall as I am and many gears. The terrain is rough: around narrow passes, some areas are straight up, others are straight down. The ride outperforms Disney World's Space Mountain.

On the ice field, everyone exits except for Evelyn. No, she will not go home with a broken hip or leg. She watches from the front of the moon buggy as everyone enjoys slip-sliding and falling.

I step one foot down on the slippery ice with colossal fanfare, like Neal Armstrong when he put his foot on the moon. We aim to walk about 200 feet to the Canadian flag on the ice. Being from Florida, I am new to walking on ice. I quickly learn to plant my heel into the ice. I start feeling very confident in my newfound walking skills. I giggle as I watch many of the others fall on the ice. But pride goes before a fall.

Like all tourists, I have my photo taken with the flag. I am bragging and boasting about how I maneuvered through the ice without slipping, and just as I am bragging to my sister, BAM! I fall so hard that my wrist

The Columbia Icefield challenges participants to race to the Canadian flag without falling. Florida native Natalie made it to the flag without a fall, but her pride met its match with a slippery tumble.

is bleeding. I return to the ice explorer crawling on my hands and knees like a baby.

I am a Floridian, and that will not change. The trip to the Canadian Rockies is a once-in-a-lifetime experience—including the $20 bowl of chili and trekking on the ice fields.

SMART TIP: Embrace the adventure, but don't be arrogant. That can make or break your day (and possibly your limbs).

TUNISIA:
The Arab Spring—We Are There

We finally arrive in Tunis, the capital of Tunisia, after barely making the last flight from Frankfurt. We thought it was from a snowstorm in the Frankfurt area. Little did we know the real reason. From Tunis, we traveled on a bus to Sousse, the "Pearl of the Sabel." We laughed and enjoyed the vendors in the market.

But a young man in a nearby rural town was not laughing. His problem had started the day before.

How the Arab Spring Started

Sidi Bouzid, Tunisia, December 16: Mohammed Bouazizi, a street vendor, borrowed $200 to buy produce to sell on the street. This was his way of making a living.

December 17: In the morning, Bouzizzi started his workday at 8:00 a.m. His produce was fresh and selling well. He was known as a popular man who gave free fruit and vegetables to poor families. However, at about 10:30 a.m., the police began harassing him for not having a vendor's permit. He did not have the money to bribe them.

Reports were that a female officer accosted Bouazizi and told him to leave because he did not have that permit. "I do not have to have a permit," he answered. At that point, she slapped him in the face, spit upon him, confiscated his electronic weighing scales, and overturned his produce cart. Confused and upset, the young man went to the governor's office to complain and get his scales back. The authorities refused to see him. He told them that he would burn himself.

One Man Statement

December 17: At 11:30 a.m., Bouazizi went to a station and bought a can of gasoline. He went back to the street in front of the governor's building. While standing in the middle of traffic, he asked, "How do you expect me to make a living?" He doused himself with gasoline and lit a match—people in the street panicked. He had burns over 90 percent of his body. They rushed him to the Ben Arous Burn and Trauma Center.

Word Spread through Social Media

Tuesday, December 21: We arrive at the desert outpost of Doug, a large oasis and gateway to the Sahara. We are doing what all tourists dream about: riding a camel. We laugh as we get on—rock and roll as we ride and take pictures when we get off. It is fun talking about it and recalling how silly we looked atop those desert beasts. All is right with the world . . . or is it?

Wednesday, December 22: We stay in a secured compound with concrete walls and guarded gates. Our wonderful guide, Kamil, told us to stay within the compound.

A fellow tourist from Atlanta plays in a rock band, and we called him "Rock Star." Natalie and Rock Star decide to walk to the edge of the desert at night to experience the splendor of a full moon. The edge of the desert is on the other side of the high wall and street. Slowly, a van with covered windows drives by. Five minutes later, the same van with covered windows stops beside them.

The driver yells in broken English, "Are you Americans?"

Rock Star yells back, "Yes."

The driver asks for their passports. Natalie can see men with machine guns peeping through the back windows of the van and starts running toward the gate of the compound across the street. The driver yells, "Get back to the compound, now!"

Saturday, December 25: We are ecstatic about the Roman ruins and a trip to an artist's paradise, a city called Sidi-Bou-Said. Something is going on. People are chit-chatting in secrecy with each other in the cafes and police are everywhere. The home of President Ben-Ali is here—and we are warned not to look in that direction.

Sunday, December 26: We are awakened to catch a 5:00 a.m. flight to Frankfurt. "Hurry, Hurry, Hurry," the driver says. "You cannot miss the flight!"

People are scurrying around, and they tell us this will be the last flight out of Tunis. We do not find out what happened in Tunisia until the next day.

International News

January 4, 2011: Mohammed Bouazizi died at 5:30 p.m. News stories everywhere told what happened in Tunisia, and that 5,000 people were shouting, "We will avenge his death!"

The actions in Tunisia spread like wildfire. The president of Tunisia resigned, along with other leaders of Arab nations. With social media, people get information quickly. We had witnessed the beginning of the Arab Spring and did not even know it.

SMART TIP: Before traveling, especially to regions experiencing political unrest or societal changes, it is important to become informed about the current events affecting those areas. Utilize resources such as the US Department of State's website at https://travel.state.gov for up-to-date travel advisories and safety information. And, always follow the directions and recommendations of your guide.

IRELAND:
I Give You No Blarney

By Natalie

I had no idea what it meant to kiss the Blarney Stone or even what it was. I assumed I would go into a room and this stone would be on a table, and I would reach over and kiss it. Boy, was I wrong!

We are traveling in beautiful Ireland. I am attracted to two things: how green everything is and how many stones are piled up. Our Irish travels have led us to Cork, Ireland's largest and southernmost county. To the northwest is the fifteenth-century Blarney Castle, home to the Blarney Stone and my exciting adventure.

We are approaching Blarney Castle. It is okay as far as castles go, but not the biggest and best. It looks like an old, run-down grey box with a tower beside it. Vines cover the walls to keep with the green theme, and evergreen trees surround them. Although there are earlier sites, a gentleman named McCarthy built the castle on the advice of a witch whose life he saved.

Many Steep, Narrow Steps

So here I am, going into the tower entrance to climb the 127 steps in a narrow hall to the tower—and I mean narrow. Evelyn, who is not so adventuresome, decides to stay at the bottom of the steps. Suddenly, she hears these cries and screams of anguish. A woman is having a panic attack. She will not continue to go up. She is frozen in place. The directors come to help. First, the people behind her must come back down, and all the ones ahead of her must continue. They slowly coax her to take one step at a time and take her for medical attention. I do not know any of this, as I am already at the top of the castle.

I must follow a narrow ledge along the wall. A small fence keeps you from falling a couple of stories. There is a short wait, and I watch other courageous people emerge from kissing this block of limestone built onto the battlements in 1446. Battlements are areas of gaps or indentations, often rectangular to allow for the launch of arrows or other projectiles.

My Turn

It is my turn. I am instructed to lie down on my back and lean backward over a gap on the edge of an eighty-five-foot drop. Thankfully, there are iron railings and assistants to help prevent accidents. I give it a little peck, lift myself out of the Blarney position, and make my way down the same narrow stairway.

As I kiss the stone, I am supposed to be endowed with the gift of eloquence and gab—which I thought I had already.

How gross is the Blarney Stone? Well, you hear lots of blarney about it. Some stories say the Blarney Stone was once part of the deflector stone at the bottom of a toilet.

The person who kisses the Blarney Stone will earn the gift of gab —and Natalie's up next, ready to recline and seal her fate with a kiss.

Some stories tell how the locals would urinate on the Blarney Stone at night and have a good laugh when tourists lined up to kiss it in the morning. These are up to you to believe or not.

Also, the word "blarney" in the dictionary is a noun and a verb. It is "talk that aims to charm, pleasantly flatter, or persuade." Supposedly, the word came into use when a member of the McCarthy family came to Queen Elizabeth I. The talkative McCarthy managed to try to talk his way to stall the queen from a siege of the castle by brilliant flattery. The queen grew exasperated and uttered something to the effect that she was hearing blarney.

And when I get home, I can tell all my friends and colleagues that I kissed the Blarney Stone. And they will say, "Wow! They have no idea of the angst and the knowledge that the stone I kissed may have been used as a toilet.

SMART TIP: When recounting your Irish adventures, don't skip the Blarney Stone—no fibs, no blarney. It's a story worth telling, complete with narrow steps, a nerve-wracking ledge, and a peck on a legendary rock.

BRAZIL:
Fishing for Piranha

By Natalie

What is the most feared creature in the Amazon? Anaconda? Jaguar? Mosquitos?

No! The most feared creature in the Amazon is the piranha—the fish with sharp, razor-like teeth that thrives on the smell of blood. The piranha is a movie star creating a feeding frenzy in every moviegoer's mind. That is one of the adventures I intend to pursue: fishing for piranha.

We arrive in Manaus, Brazil, the jungle paradise the rubber barons created. This boom of the nineteenth and early twentieth centuries produced 90 percent of the world's supply of rubber, and wealthy rubber barons to go along with it. But a sneaky Englishman smuggled seeds to plant rubber trees in Asia, and the barons lost their fortunes. They left behind some fabulous mansions, an opera house, and tales of intrigue. One myth is about a fish that can eat an entire man in less than five seconds.

Fish Excitement

"Everyone who wants to go fishing for piranha—grab your gear," shouts Conrado, our Brazilian guide. He is a professional bull rider in his spare time, going everywhere on the riding circuit. So, I guess fishing for piranha is tame compared to his other job.

My enthusiasm is jarring. Catching piranha . . . can you imagine? Five of us transfer to a small, motorized dinghy. We are on the Rio Negro River from Manaus. The river is calm; there is no wind. We enter a small tributary under a dense canopy with trees as tall as the Empire State Building, vines as thick as a Sumo wrestler's leg, and leaves like umbrellas at the beach. Piranhas thrive in shallow banks along these tributaries where fruit, insects, and small animals fall from the trees.

Conrado hands us a bamboo pole with a hook and a small fish. He demonstrates how to jiggle it in the water, sloshing up and down. One fisherman observes this is not how they fish in Tennessee, where you must be quiet. But Conrado reminds him that he is not in Tennessee and is fishing for piranha, which like a lot of noise and commotion.

No Fish Tale

I am determined to win the contest to catch the most piranhas. I put my line in and slosh vigorously in the water weeds. The piranha gets the fish but not the hook. I try again, and again, and finally, I pull in my buddy. He has a small, flattened body with a red belly and a protruding jaw. But oh, those nasty choppers! Conrado knows how to pick him up. I see needle-like, triangular teeth from a horror movie biting at me. I am ready to try again, but the sun is beginning to set, and it is time to go. I do not win the contest; the guy who fished in Tennessee caught six.

What is the most feared member of the animal kingdom? Yes, piranha. Natalie is thrilled to go fishing and determined to catch the most. She catches one.

We go back to our large ship and tell our fantastic fish stories. The next night, we have a choice of entrees for dinner: deep-fried battered piranha, boiled piranha, or piranha stew, but no piranha dessert.

SMART TIP: Brazil's native tongue is Portuguese. They may walk by you and make a sound like a pig. Don't be insulted; they are saying hello, which is "oi" in Portuguese.

SAUDI ARABIA:
The Mysterious Man

Dr. Donna Robinson, as told to Evelyn

It is dusk and the end of the day during Ramadan; everyone is out, and it is complete chaos. The traffic is terrible. No one pays attention to lights or any traffic rules. Donna and four colleagues from the Royal Hospital in Riyadh decided to go to town. She is dressed in a full abaya, covering everything except her face. Donna looks around, and her colleagues are lost in the crowd. She sees them across the street, but the traffic is terrible. She is by herself. What is she to do?

The cars whiz by, and the crowds jostle Donna. Suddenly, a huge man walks up behind her and says, "Looks like you are lost."

Donna explains that her friends are across the street and that she is scared to cross.

He says, "I'll walk you across."

The huge man steps into the street, holds up his hand, and traffic stops. It is like Moses parting the water at the Red Sea crossing: cars stopped, and they go across.

The huge man says, "I give you my card, and if you ever need help, give them this card."

Donna thanks him and soon spots her friends. She has no idea what the card says or who the man was. One day, she will find out.

Donna Goes to Arabia

How did Donna get to a place like Saudi Arabia? She is a clinical nurse specialist in high-risk obstetrics. The hospital serving the royal family was seeing an undue number of deaths among the children and mothers. They needed help, and Donna was in the right place at the right time. She interviewed, got the job, and took off to the unknown.

Six Weeks of Cultural Immersion

She had six weeks of cultural immersion. The class had people from about fifty nationalities, many from Muslim countries. Donna was the only one from the US.

They taught some essential Arabic words and how to read common signs. They were warned to have absolutely nothing religious on them—except for Islamic items. You can have no symbols, crosses, or jewelry that is religious in any way. They can have no pork—not even pictures of pigs in a book. No movies are allowed.

You must have everything covered: the arms and feet must be hidden with no part showing. Donna wears tennis shoes the whole time she is there. Never sit with your feet or legs crossed, and never, never show the soles of your shoes. Prayer is five times a day and is called by a muezzin from the minaret, and it is loud. You must stop what you are doing during the prayer call.

Donna, a flexible person, adjusts to Saudi life, although life in the hospital compound is as much as she was used to. So, she does experience freedom as long as she does not stray too far.

Taking a Walk

After weeks of exposure to Saudi culture, she decides to walk to the store. At the entrance to the store, a woman is begging (unusual for a female). She steps up to give her some coins. Bam! She is hit from behind by a man with a long, scruffy beard, who shouts, *Haram! Haram!* (forbidden). Donna, who has had to defend herself, swings back at him. (Haram!) He summons a nearby policeman and wants her put in jail for Haram! A woman cannot hit a man.

Then, Donna remembers the card the huge man had given her some time ago. She produces it and tells the policeman how this gentleman said to use it if she was ever in trouble. They look at the card and freeze! The man who attacked her runs. The policeman tells her to go ahead. She gives the beggar woman the money and returns to the hospital complex.

She inquires, "Who was this guy that made the traffic stop? Who was this guy that froze everyone?"

They find out he is in charge of the division that makes people disappear for the King. That card is worth its weight in gold.

Donna loves working there and especially likes the ordinary people. She went there for a six-month assignment and stayed for three years.

SMART TIP: Dive into the dos and don'ts of your destination's culture before you take off. Being well-prepared can turn potential pitfalls into smooth sailing, whether it's understanding local customs or mastering essential phrases. You may not have the opportunity for cultural immersion, but you can at least Google cultural training for _____(whatever country you are visiting).

PART 2

Love of Cultural Enrichment

Diverse thought and traditions of other areas.
Understanding how other people live and think.
Travel is yoga for the brain.

CHINA:
Traditional Chinese Medicine

By Evelyn

1999 I am in a park in Beijing. A gentle breeze is flowing through the bodies of twenty men and women dressed in white tops. Am I seeing this in slow motion? Are my eyes deceiving me? A few stop briefly to glance at the American foreigners passing by, and then, as a quiet cloud descends, they continue their dream-like movements.

I am interested and must learn more about this healthy activity. I have heard of Chi, the life force that is the basis of traditional Chinese medicine. But I had never seen it in person; now it's everywhere. I am observing an ancient practice that originated as an ancient martial art in China called Tai Chi. However, over the years, the practice has been more focused on health promotion and rehabilitation. According to Chinese philosophy, this deliberative pace helps to promote the circulation of blood, fluids, and chi life force energy through the body.

Tai Chi is one aspect of Chinese medicine. What else can I expect from Chinese medicine? Stay tuned!!

To the Traditional Chinese Hospital and Medical School

"We are going to a Chinese medical school," our director says.

Several others think *big deal* and do not share my excitement. I am thrilled just thinking about visiting the medical school and learning about Chinese medicine from the practitioners. Natalie had slept wrong, and the muscles in her neck are paining her. She does not share my enthusiasm but thinks maybe they can help her.

We approach a large white building with most of its windows open. There are no air conditioners, and it is hot in July. A short but muscular doctor in a white coat greets us.

He starts his lecture: "Traditional Chinese medicine goes back to the Qin dynasty and the "Yellow Emperor," he says.

I am so excited to hear about this leader and, later, the idea of Chi—the life force—and, later, yin and yang. A guy from Texas yawns. Some ladies look around at strange drawings on the wall. Natalie is still in pain.

He continues his hour-long lecture on herbal medicine, acupuncture, moxibustion, the Chinese philosophy of surgery, diet, and exercise. What a thrill. Sure, it is hot, but I want more and even ask a few questions. A lady from Minnesota eyes me with daggers.

And now comes the time for analysis. We were given a brochure with all the herbal remedies for any ailment. He continues, "More than 800 kinds of herb medicines are prepared in ready-to-use form. More than 260 kinds of patent medicine in the form of pills, powder, ream, dan (drug-soaked in ribbon gauze), tincture, or oil solutions."

The medical school gives us a proven secret recipe from famous old specialists. The first one on the list is Yan Nian Yi Shou Wan, made from ginseng and pilose antlers. It is suitable for male infertility, impotence, polyuria, and other ailments regarding the male genitalia.

Participants are invited to fill out the form. Guess who asks for one: Tex and the lady from Minnesota. Tex buys about fifty pills for his ailments at the cost of $200.

I especially enjoy seeing the charts for acupuncture at the medical school. Although to me, the charts look like mixed-up spaghetti, I have found that many people have found healing, especially for muscular pain, with this procedure.

CHINA: Traditional Chinese Medicine   53

Natalie asks if anything can be done to relieve the pain in her shoulder. "Come with me," he says. "We will do electric massage."

He hooks her up and sends the electric charge, and the pain she had felt disappears, but new pains from the electric charge appear.

After the exciting visit to the medical school (for me, anyway), we go to a traditional Chinese dinner of Peking duck and all the trimmings. It is time to retire and look forward to the visit to the Beijing Zoo and the giant pandas.

There is great excitement at breakfast, especially the anticipation of seeing the pandas. One downside is that Tex and some others were sick the night before. I don't know if it was from all the pills that he took at once or the Peking duck.

How pleasing it was to go to medical school. Despite our problems, I am still interested in studying Chinese medicine, which many have found very beneficial.

Meet Beijing Zoo's star ambassador of Chinese heritage. Fresh from a bamboo feast, the panda is the ultimate symbol of conservation efforts.

SMART TIP #1: Learning about medicine from other cultures is pertinent today. We have lots of options, but please stick to your doctor. Remember—as the Chinese professor told us—these are secret remedies that have not been proven, like our medicines, which must meet rigorous standards.

SMART TIP #2: Make a medical emergency kit that includes your needs. It is especially important if you are going overseas. See our suggestions for a kit in the back pages of this book.

FRANCE:
Is Mona Lisa Still Smiling?

Have you ever wondered why Mona Lisa has such a mysterious smile? What is she thinking? Why is her portrait one of the most popular in the world?

For our first trip overseas, we travel for three weeks with an overland group. Our second stop during the tour is Paris and the hotel is on the outskirts, away from everything. But we are determined to see the Louvre and the Mona Lisa.

We are pretty adventuresome and brave the Paris subway to the museum. When entering the Louvre, we ask for directions to where the Mona Lisa is displayed, and they point us to a hall. A few people are scattered about looking at other paintings. We see three or four gathered on the right-hand side. Here we are at Leonardo's masterpiece. It is a lot smaller than we thought it would be. However, as interested art students, we can admire portraits for the first time.

Oh, look at her dress. It is embroidered with tiny, intricate loops I have never noticed in pictures. Hey, look at her hands, how relaxed they are. And yes, we have heard Leonardo loved rocky landscapes, but these are different. The painting of the horizon on the right is higher, offering a bird's eye view of the rocks; the one on the left is much lower with flowing water. There is no way these two could meet if we could peep behind her head. Could this have something to do with the mysterious smile? The left background appears to pull the eye down; the right side seems to push it up. Are we imagining that she is about to break into a smile? How great it is to see this painting up close and personal and to be able to note and discuss details.

Surprisingly, this small painting has inspired poetry, songs, paintings, sculptures, novels, movies, myths, forgeries, and theft. Are you warm? Are you real? Is Mona Lisa a real person, or just a cold and lonely lovely work of art?

Our Second Trip to Paris

Our second trip to Paris in 2015 is also with a travel company, and the tour includes the Louvre. We rush to where the Mona Lisa is hung. But, to our surprise, she is not there. We are told by a docent that she has been moved to a larger room, which she shares with the Italian master painter Caravaggio. No one pays attention to—they are all excited about Mona Lisa—holding cell phones and cameras up over the heads of the crowd. We are pushed and pulled and lucky to get out.

We never get close to the Mona Lisa the second time we visit. We did not even get to see if she is still smiling. Can she endure all the flashes and adoration for over 500 years and maintain that smile? I assume that she will.

SMART TIP: The best time to visit Mona Lisa or museums is when they first open. Other times to visit are either during midday, which could be lunchtime in most countries, or at the end of the business day.

CANADA: Calgary Stampede and Head-Smashed-In Buffalo Jump

By Evelyn

Ride 'em, cowboy! Yippie-ti-ta-yeh! Whoopee! Attaboy! Go! We are in Calgary, Alberta, Canada, the week just before the Great Calgary Stampede. This is the roughest, toughest Western festival and is billed as the world's largest outdoor rodeo. For ten days, cowboys and girls face off riding bucking broncos, hanging onto wild bulls, and speeding around barrels.

We catch the spirit. We see the chuckwagons and are invited to a free pancake breakfast with everyone in the downtown area. Over a million people will be here for the parade, stage shows, concerts, chuckwagon racing, and First Nations competition. And to think, this grand celebration has been going on since 1912.

Tower in Calgary

We are not there for the stampede but to take a Western Canada tour. First, we visit Calgary Tower, which rises high above the city and offers a must-see view. We zip up the elevator to the observation deck, where you can see the Rocky Mountains, the foothills, and the prairies.

In the middle of the observation tower is a line of people standing to see downtown. Why are these people in line and taking selfies? They are stepping on a solid, transparent platform of glass with a see-through floor. What? No way—it is too frightening. What if you have acrophobia—fear of heights? I try to convince myself that I am not afraid. My daughter Sharlene says that she knows a way. You turn away, back in, and don't look down; that way, you conquer fear. Does it work? Natalie walks out with her eyes closed until the glass wall stops her. She then holds on to the railing for dear life.

Welcome to Calgary, the thrilling home of the legendary Stampede. Climb the tower and step onto the glass floor—an exhilarating view that'll make your heart race almost as much as the rodeo below.

Trip to Drumheller

One great perk of traveling is meeting people who have also traveled. They will give you ideas. A couple we met on one trip told us that if you go to Calgary, you must go to Drumheller. We had never heard of it. So we added this trip.

Drumheller is the dinosaur capital of the world. You know you are there because there are dinosaur statues everywhere.

To think that dinosaurs roamed a lush sub-tropical habitat some million years ago gives us pause as we look at Horseshoe Canyon. These are the Canadian badlands with maroon-striped canyon walls. It is a site to behold. Tall, skinny spires of rock called hoodoos result from thousands of years of erosion. They look like tall, skinny men with little flat-top hats. This funny-sounding name is derived from

Hoodoo spirituality, in which certain natural forms of names are said to possess magical powers.

The Royal Terrell Museum has one of the world's largest collections of dinosaur bones. You can even tour the laboratory where the finds are assembled. We have never seen so many bones.

Head-Smashed-in Buffalo Jump

In many areas of the West, the native people would catch buffalo not by shooting them but by running them off a cliff. This is an old practice; researchers who have used radiocarbon dating believe this was an active jump at least 5,500 years ago. The Natives encircled the herd and, wearing wolf skins, crept closer and closer. The buffalo, thinking they were real wolves, would start to run. The scouts drove them toward the cliff, and when they got there, they had no alternative but to jump off. In the blink of an eye, they obtained more food in a single moment than anyone else in human history.

How did the jump get this name? It comes from the Blackfoot name Estipah-skikkini-kots, or "head-smashed-in." According to the Blackfoot legend, a young boy wanted to watch from below while the animals jumped off the cliff. The elders warned him, but he stole away and hid.

The little boy at the bottom watched but soon was overwhelmed. When the buffalo carcasses were hauled away, the boy was found with his head smashed in.

Amazingly, these natives used their skills to outsmart animals for food and sustenance.

SMART TIP: When traveling, don't forget your binoculars. These invaluable tools will not only enhance your appreciation of the site's historical significance, but will also provide a closer look at the remarkable skill and ingenuity of the ancient hunters. Be sure to visit the tourist center, which brings the past to life.

MOROCCO:
The Little Sales Boy

By Natalie

Tangier, Casablanca, and Marrakesh stir mystery, excitement, and a hint of spice in the air. We are in Tangier, a city built on the slopes of the white chalk cliffs above the Mediterranean Sea. The intrigue of the movie *Casablanca* haunts us.

We check into the Hotel Continental, built in 1870, which has a guest book full of notables. We even stay in a fancy suite with a wall plaque that reads, "Prime Minister Winston Churchill stayed in this room."

So, with all this history and mystery, what do we tell people when we get home? We may mention the casbah and the hotel, but the story of the little sales boy of Morocco dominates.

In many countries of the Middle East, street salespeople, peddlers, or hawkers descend the minute unsuspecting tourists step out of their vehicles. In *Murder on the Nile,* Agatha Christie describes these guys as "pesky mosquitoes." They have passed their trade secrets on to successive generations who are skilled in their work.

Mother and I are walking along, and one young man approaches her.

"Want to buy bracelet?" He dangles several in her face.

"No," she says and smiles.

"Want to buy necklace?" He insists.

"No, thank you," she states with all her Southern charm, trying not to be rude.

"Want to buy drum?" Now he is in her face again.

I have had enough. In my loudest voice, I say NO! LEAVE US ALONE!!

The boy looks at my mother and sweetly says about me, "She is not happy. She must be happy."

And I proceeded to say, "I would be happy if you would go away and leave us alone." He leaves.

We get back on the bus, and who do we see? That young man is outside our window, showing that drum. I continue to ignore him.

I say to Mother, "I will be right back."

I leave the bus. After a few minutes, I return to the bus with that drum, which is prominent in my display case today. When I wave goodbye to him, several of his friends are beside him, trying to sell their own goods.

We learn that when encountering peddlers, no matter what age they may be, it's best to avoid engaging with them. A simple "no" often gets misinterpreted as an invitation to bargain. To minimize interaction, adopt a zombie-like expression and avoid making eye contact as you pass by. You can't smile or strike up a conversation with them. Should you decide to purchase something, like I did when purchasing the drum, know how to negotiate a price. We never pay the set price. I start way below half the ask with a limit in mind. I walk away until I get the price I'm willing to pay. I keep small bills in my pocket. After the sale, be prepared for other peddlers to take note. They often share information about generous travelers.

SMART TIP: It's crucial to keep your cash hidden to avoid becoming a target for theft. Additionally, be wary of seemingly free offerings. For example, while in Tunisia, we were offered soft drinks as we mounted our camels; as soon as we opened them, the vendors demanded payment. Remember, nothing comes without a price.

ICELAND:
Trip to the Moon

By Evelyn

"Look, Natalie," I say as we land in Reykjavik. "The landscape looks just like pictures from the moon."

And it does! Iceland is the most moon-like place on Earth. Calderas, ash cones, steaming volcanic vents, cinders, pumice, and various lava flows are found both here and on the moon, all without vegetation.

This is so real that in the 1960s, NASA brought the Apollo astronauts to train in Iceland for the similar terrain and the rocks. Iceland's dense, dark basaltic rocks are as close to moon rocks as most of us will ever see.

Iceland is an excellent place for travelers. You can relax in the Blue Lagoon and follow the Golden Circle, which takes you to geothermal wonders, waterfalls, and historical spots around Reykjavik. We especially like Strokkur, Iceland's most active geyser. We have seen many geysers, from Yellowstone to New Zealand, but the exciting thing about this one is that you can get close to it. We have to run to keep from getting sprayed.

Out of This World

We always enjoy the interesting "touristy" places, but what is the country like? What are the people like? What is the history of the place? We find this out by talking to locals. The guides are good, but if you can find a local to share their knowledge, that is the best way to get inside interesting information. We find Ingrid, an Icelandic gem. She talks about a culture unusual to most Americans; maybe out of this world.

"Hallo," Ingrid greets us. That is easy enough. It is similar to English, only it is "hah-lo," with the accent on the last syllable. Other than that, the language is a mystery. It is derived from old Norse and developed from the early Vikings and Norsemen who came 1,150 years ago. However, because of isolation, it is strikingly different from other Scandinavian languages today. Most of the people also speak English.

What's in a Name

Ingrid informs us of some interesting things about Iceland. Babies remain nameless for weeks or even months after they are born, and their special name is a top secret until their christening. Until then, the child is given a cutesy name like Lilli, meaning little princess or sweet boy. And then the names can be confusing—all the members of an Icelandic family may have different last names.

When the country was settled, Icelanders used a patronymic (or increasingly matronymic) system, the Nordic system. The child's last name is made by taking the first name of the father or mother and adding son—if a boy or dottir—if a girl. For example, Karl's son would be Karlsson; his daughter's last name would be Karlsdottir. The Icelandic Naming Committee and the Personal Names Committee keep an official record of all names; it must approve all new given (first) names. So, the baby's name must be approved before christening. Some names are illegal. You would not want to name a child something that might cause them harm or disgrace, like Satan. Also, you could not include Camilla because the letter "C" is not in the Icelandic alphabet.

Ingrid shows us a telephone book. All people are listed alphabetically by their first name. Then comes the last name, their profession, and their home address. And the profession can be quite creative. Suppose you want to be a sorcerer or a circus performer; you could list that as your profession. How about being a gunfighter?

Folklore is Real

This striking land of supernatural beauty is matched by rich and extensive folklore and superstitions. According to Ingrid, most people believe in supernatural beings, especially the Huldufolk: hidden people or elves. Local elves can stop road work if they are angry, Ingrid informs us. She tells the story of a street that is being paved; it angered the elves and so now the street ends abruptly with the paved road and immediately becomes the regular road. These huldufolk have special holidays to bring them out of hiding. They are especially active during New Year's Eve, Twelfth Night, or Christmas Night, and you might want to leave food out for them. If you are interested, you can go to Elf School in Reykjavik to learn about the thirteen types of elves.

We especially like stories about trolls. I remember reading the fairy tale "The Three Billy Goats Gruff and the Troll." According to legend, trolls are real in Iceland. Vic is a beautiful beach with black sand, but above the shore is a basalt rock formation called Reynisdrangar. The story goes that this is a real troll who was caught by sunlight trying to drag ships onto shore.

And for all of you with birthdays coming up soon, you do not get cakes, candles, or presents if you live in Iceland. You must do the opposite and give the party for all of your friends, give them presents, and pay for it all. Which way do you prefer?

SMART TIP: While Iceland's natural wonders may steal the show, take the time to explore the lives of the people and rich their folklore. From learning about the language and naming customs to delving into tales of elves and trolls, you'll find that Iceland is a journey to the moon and back—a truly otherworldly experience waiting to be discovered.

COSTA RICA:
Fruit Bowl of the World

Pura Vida (translated as pure life or simple life) is the most famous saying of the Ticos, names given to Costa Rica by themselves and other Spanish speakers. They get this because, in speaking, they tend to add the diminutive "tico" to the end of words.

Costa Rica, a country that has been a friend of the United States and a beacon of democracy in Central and South America, has great beaches, luxuriant rain forests, magnificent volcanoes, and interesting animals. During the colonial period, Costa Rica was among the poorest and isolated from the Spanish Empire. The Spanish killed off natives who lived in the area. The rainforest was not a desirable place to settle, so you will not see the colonial towns like in neighboring countries.

We fly into San Jose, the capital. This was not a colonial city; nevertheless, San Jose has a national theater, national museum, cathedral, congress, and Supreme Court, all of which are from the nineteenth century or later but are still quite beautiful.

King Coffee

We are on a coffee plantation. It is early December, just the right time to pick coffee. "Okay, we are going to have a coffee-picking contest, and the winner gets a prize. Here are the rules: the beans you pick must be red, or they will not count. You will put them in a basket, and you will have fifteen minutes to pick," the guide says.

Natalie, the inveterate competitor, enters the contest, determined to win. Five minutes—going as fast as she can; 10 minutes—putting on the speed—time's up! Let's weigh. Did Natalie win? The suspense grows. Another competitor barely beats her.

Coffee is king in Costa Rica. Ox carts were used to transport bags from the fields to the factory. At first, they were simple wooden structures. But then, artists began decorating and designing the carts, especially the huge wheels. For over a century, one town, Sarchi, has made these colorful and decorative oxcarts. We visit the factory, where all of the work is hand-painted, elaborate, and beautiful.

Want a Tarantula?

We are going to the Tortuguero National Park and the Pachira Lodge. We move slowly through the waterways, looking for turtles, caymans, herons, toucans, egrets, and monkeys. The latter are abundant. From our knowledge of monkeys at Silver Springs, Florida, we emphasize with the guides not to feed or try to pet the monkeys. They will bite. We experience howler monkeys that howl all night and leave their remains on the handrails along the walks. Watch your hands!

We have a morning boat ride to the Sarapiqui area and tour the La Silva Biological Station. It is here on a high bluff that Natalie encounters a tarantula. The instructor shows us a fish tank with tarantulas. He puts his hand in and brings one of the tarantulas out, and he asks who

Tarantula Alert! Costa Rica's lush wilderness teems with diverse wildlife, including some seriously impressive spiders. Here's Natalie bravely handling a tarantula—but remember, only under expert supervision.

would like to hold it. Natalie, ever the brave one, volunteers. And while she looks, talks to, and watches the tarantula on her hand, he educates us about spiders. This one is harmless; others are not.

We leave for the Tilajari Resort Area and Rain Forest Reserve. We take a float trip on the Penas Blancas River and look for sloths, iguanas, crocodiles, and numerous tropical birds. That night, we see the Arenal Volcano with glowing lava running down its sides.

Costa Rica is Latin America's most stable, progressive, and prosperous nation. It abolished its army in 1949, making it the only sovereign nation without an army. Costa Rica has a better record of human development than other regions.

SMART TIP: Many Americans leave the United States to live or retire in other countries like Costa Rica. If you consider this, investigate the country's government, sustainability, stability, cost of living, housing, and health care.

ECUADOR: Standing on Two Sides of the Equator

The kinkajou, or "honey bear," is an exotic animal in the Ecuadorian rain forest. It is also something people "ooh" and "ahh" about and want as pets. Our friend Anna got this adorable animal from Ecuador and took it home. One day, she left the kinkajou in a cage while she went to work. But he broke out of the cage and ransacked the house. Every bit of stuffing in the sofa and chairs was ripped out and pantries were raided. Flour, cornmeal, and potato chips were all over the floor. This charmer belongs in the rainforest, not in someone's house.

Ecuador is trying to protect its wildlife, but it is difficult with those in the illegal market selling exotic pets. In 2008, Ecuador's Constitution was the first in the world to recognize the Rights of Nature and ecosystems. Known for its rich ecology, we were eager to see such a place and visit the rainforest.

Presidential Speech

We arrive in Quito, the capital of Ecuador, a city 9,300 feet above sea level. Marco, our guide, shows us a few places, then says, "I want to take you to hear President Rafael Correa giving his weekly speech (in Spanish)."

He leads us to the plaza as we zigzag through the crowds. We stand as they sing their national anthem (it is beautiful). A large group of people start protesting against the president, and Marco whisks us away from the crowd. The demonstration is quickly managed. Several years later, we learn that the president served for ten years and was exiled from the country for alleged bribery and corruption.

Standing on Both Sides of the Equator

This imaginary line is equidistant between the North Pole and the South Pole. About 24,901 miles long, it divides the Earth between the Northern and Southern Hemispheres.

We are at Mitad del Mundo, a small village where the Monument to the Equator stands. It is shaped like a pyramid, with each side facing a cardinal direction and topped with a globe. Evelyn plants her left foot in the Southern hemisphere and her right foot in the Northern hemisphere. Natalie walks the Equator line like she is on a balance beam.

Otavalo: an Indigenous City

A famous market called the Otavalo Market is in this town. We buy several pieces of beautiful fabrics and hand-painted crafts. One of the neat items that we observe is a Huaorani blow gun, and we watch as natives demonstrate how to blow darts to track animals.

To the Orphanage

We want to experience how Ecuadorians help each other. Natalie is interested in visiting an orphan home, so Marco pivots from the scripted schedule and takes us to a small orphanage. The leaders and teachers are accommodating and allow the children to greet us—even in the middle of class. We sit together on a step and speak broken Spanish as they laugh at us. What a great ending to our trip to Ecuador.

SMART TIP: Keep your distance from public demonstrations and protestors. Do not participate. While they are an educational experience to watch, they can quickly get out of hand.

EL SALVADOR:
Walk a Mile in their Shoes

The greatest surprise we encountered while traveling was El Salvador. Although the stories about it are not too optimistic, the infrastructure is surprising. We feel as safe there as in any foreign country (never let up your guard anywhere). President Salvatore Ceren, elected in June 2014, made many promises, and transportation has greatly improved here.

We travel through colonial cities and spend little time in San Salvador, the capital. We meet our guide, Alejandro (Alex), who will accompany us throughout El Salvador. We do not even recognize many of these cities today, which were so crucial in the past. Alex informs us that El Salvador has only about 2 percent natives; most of the people are mestizos—Spanish and natives mixed—and it has been this way for generations.

Suchitoto

The first town is Suchitoto, which you have probably never heard of, but it is beautiful. Typically built in the plaza style, it has a gleaming white cathedral, government offices, and small shops. It is also the location of the most luxurious boutique hotel we have ever visited, Los Almendros de San Lorenzo, a restored colonial building.

The hotel encompasses several buildings around a vast courtyard with a fountain. We are taken to a gigantic hotel room. When you enter the room, you are greeted by a lion fountain with water pouring out of its mouth and flowing into a jacuzzi. The mega-king bed has an ornate headboard. Across from this is a spacious sitting room with elaborate colonial furniture.

El Salvador was involved in a terrible civil war between communists and the government from 1979 to 1992. It was terrible for the people, with death squads on both sides. So, these courageous people turned to art. White stucco buildings were painted brilliant pink, blue, and yellow. They would add faces, birds, and other things from nature. The art is indeed a spectacle.

Indigo Gold

Spaniards did not find gold here, but instead found the indigo plant. We are invited to participate in the dyeing process. Short, oval leaves from the indigo tree have been collected, blended, and added to water. The color is not blue but a yellowish brown. We are given a white scarf to be twisted and submerged in the dye for thirty minutes. As we wait, we learn about the history and importance of indigo. Then we air dry our scarves and rinse them in cold water. Next, we hand wash them in a mild soap and dry in the sunlight. And voila; we have our tie-dyed scarves.

The last night, we get a call from the company's owners. They want to take us to a local place for a traditional dish. The owners are delightful and order pupusas, a corn pancake filled with bean, cheese, and meat.

Alex tells us of his dreams. He wants to develop tours to explore archaeological sites like Joya de Ceren, known as the Pompeii of the Americas. It is a pre-Columbian farming village thirty-six miles north of San Salvador. About 600 AD, the volcano Loma Caldera erupted, burying the site in ash. Scholars have excavated the town, which is classified as a UNESCO World Heritage site.

SMART TIP: Do not judge people until you have walked a mile in their shoes and do not judge a country until you have had an opportunity to visit; the impressions from news stories may be biased or may refer to only one place or area.

COLOMBIA:
Thumbs Up to Colombia

When you think of Colombia, what comes to mind? Drug cartels? Danger?

Before our trip to Colombia, Natalie went to a doctor to ask about the safety concerns of a colonoscopy. The doctor, who knew of her plans to travel to Colombia, replied, "It is safer to have a colonoscopy than to go to Colombia." He had read the news.

Colombia has received a bum rap from the press, and like any country in the world, there are places where tourists should not travel. But what you may miss by not visiting this beautiful country may surprise you. There are modern cities with skyscrapers. The country has one of the highest college graduate rates and speaks the purest classic Spanish.

We fly into Bogota, where modern skyscrapers meet history. Our first jaunt in Bogota is "touristy." We go to the plaza, the standard design of Spain and its former colonies. There is a statue of Simon Bolivar with the usual pigeons perched on his head; he liberated South America from Spain in 1821, and had visions of a United States of South America. That did not work.

Now, we are ready for our second stop, from Bogota to the coffee triangle of Pereira. We meet Claudia and Julion, our guide and driver.

As we are traveling along the mountainous terrain, we see a smiling soldier standing next to the side of the road with his thumbs up to us. We wave back to him.

About ten miles later, we see another smiling soldier with his thumbs up on the side of the road. These soldiers are sure friendly.

Up and down these mountainous roads, we see the friendly soldiers with their thumbs up. We have never seen soldiers on the side of the road expressing so much happiness. Why are they happy we ask? Our guide explains the danger of these roads just a few years ago. The thumbs up assures us that the area and roads are safe to travel.

We reach our overnight place, the Hotel Boutique Sazaqua. This place was once part of a large hacienda but has become a boutique hotel. We love boutique hotels and request them when possible. We go to a coffee plantation on the side of a mountain with fog rolling in. Now, it is our turn to learn how to grind different types of coffee.

Our third leg is to Santa Marta, the oldest city in South America, founded in 1517. Again, we are in a gorgeous boutique hotel with two huge rooms close to the town plaza. We are there when they were preparing for the Little Sister Festival. Our guide, Alexander (we call Alexander the Great), tells us about the legend of Tomasita, who was washing her clothes by the river when a caiman ate her. The caiman is similar to an alligator and crocodile. Father asked her sister, "Where is your little sister?"

She replied, "A caiman ate my little sister." So, every January 20, there is the Little Sister Festival in Santa Marta.

Next, we go to a very crowded Cartagena. It is a haven for cruise ships, enabling tourists to say they have been in Colombia.

Returning to Bogota, we reflect on our time in Colombia. Perhaps the most profound revelation comes from our encounters with the friendly soldiers, whose thumbs-up reassures us of Colombia's remarkable transformation. These roads were fraught with danger just a decade ago, but today, they stand as symbols of Colombia's resilience and determination to embrace a brighter future.

SMART TIP: When planning your Colombian adventure, consider immersing yourself in the charm of boutique hotels, where history meets hospitality. And remember, behind every thumbs-up lies a story of hope and progress—a testament to Colombia's enduring spirit of resilience and warmth.

GUATEMALA:
Land of Eternal Spring

By Evelyn

Thud. The motor of our boat stops abruptly. The only sounds are the frantic whir as the driver tries to crank the engine and the lapping water as we dip from one wave to another. We are in Lake Atitlan, 1,000 feet deep, and pitching up and down like a tiny piece of flotsam. We do not think of this as a problem because we are entranced by the volcano rising over the village of Santiago. We think of the stories of hidden Mayan cities beneath the deep lake created by volcanic activity many moons ago.

We do not have time to worry because we are soon on the move, reflecting on our experiences in this Land of Eternal Spring.

It is only a short flight from Miami to Guatemala City. We ride over bumpy roads to Antigua, our favorite city.

Lake Atitlán's tranquil waters hold mysterious secrets—rumor has it, an ancient city lies submerged beneath.

Antigua

We stop at the end of the wide cobblestone street at the unimpressive Porta Hotel. Like many places in Central America, outdoor looks can be deceiving. We enter one of the most beautiful courtyards with a vast swimming pool, hibiscus, oleander, and tropical plants. Scarlet macaws and toucans call to us. The rooms are spacious and comfortable.

Built in the sixteenth century, Antigua is a UNESCO World Heritage Site surrounded by three volcanoes and has neatly painted colonial buildings. It was the capital of the Spanish colony until a series of earthquakes prompted the move to Guatemala City in 1776.

Our guide, Estuardo (Stu), takes us through the cathedrals, monastery ruins, and places of rulers. While sitting in the plaza, we are impressed by the industry of shoe-shine boys who want to shine our shoes—although we are wearing sandals and tennis shoes.

Market, Lakes, and More Volcanoes

From Antigua, we leave behind the colonial world and travel to the indigenous country in the highlands, known for coffee and corn. The blackened cones of thirty volcanoes dot this country, some smoking.

In this area, people live in tiny houses with tin roofs. The roof is a problem, according to Stu. The people cook and heat with an open fire, and smoke fills the house because there is no chimney. The number one cause of death and sickness among people, especially children, is a respiratory illness. The male farmers have four things they value in this order: (1) their land and crops, (2) their pickup trucks, (3) gold in their teeth, and (4) the education of their children.

He adds, "The people are poor but not miserable; there is a difference."

The whitewashed town of Chichicastenago is famous for its market, colorful cemetery, and festivals. We have been to many markets, but these young girls tug at our hearts. We are told that if we do not want to buy, we should ignore them or bargain. I am not good at ignoring or bargaining. Therefore, I have a cadre of young girls following me around saying, "Please buy from me. I made these myself."

I buy ten and stop only when I remember the volume of my suitcase.

Guatemala City

The Spaniards who settled in the lower part of Guatemala intermarried with the indigenous population, and these people forged a better lifestyle. We go through several high-end, gated communities, which contrast with the tin-covered dwellings of the countryside. Here, social customs are European. However, people moving to seek a better life often find more poverty.

Change may be coming. Stu says real change in Guatemala is one to two generations away. We ponder that potential. Here is a country with a gorgeous landscape, Mayan ruins, and Spanish colonial treasures. It is indeed a land of eternal seeking.

SMART TIP: It is difficult to keep up with the political situations in these Central American countries. However, Guatemala is generally stable, and visiting there is a must, especially the colorful city of Antigua.

ARUBA, BONAIRE, AND CURACAO: A-B-Cs of the Southern Caribbean

Want to see the Dutch in the New World? These islands are almost on the coast of Venezuela and just below the hurricane belt. They have gorgeous beaches that appeal to all types of water sports enthusiasts. But best of all, they have magnificent culture, history, and traditions.

These three islands became part of the Netherlands and the Dutch West Indies and are known as A-B-C.

"A" Stands for Aruba

If you are ever in Aruba and lose your sense of direction, look for the divi-divi tree, a natural compass that always points in a southwest direction. Many cacti grow on this island—more than you would ever want to see.

In the capital of Oranjestad, you will see ornate buildings like the ones in Amsterdam.

This Dutch colony abides by Dutch law. When an American student, Natalie Holloway, disappeared, the investigation was complicated and complex. According to our guide, the laws in Aruba are unusual. For example, if people break into your house and you lay a hand on them, you go to jail for assault. If criminals are locked in your house, you must call the police within two hours or you will be charged with kidnapping. It is legal to drink and drive. Many say that criminals have more rights than citizens here.

"B" is for Bonaire

This was our favorite island. Although it is a special municipality, it is still under Dutch law. The Spanish decided these islands were unusable and moved all the natives to work elsewhere. Then, they brought them back to work with domesticated animals, including cattle, donkeys, horses, pigs, and sheep. A tourist attraction is the wild donkey colony.

If you want a strange language, try Papiamento. It is a mixture of African, Portuguese, English, Dutch, Spanish, and native dialects.

Rincon, the oldest village in Bonaire, is inland and away from pirates. The houses are old, with unusual cactus fences. No one tries to climb over your fence.

The Dutch wanted this island for their West India trade. They defeated the Spanish and built their capital, Khalendijk. They found a commodity more precious than gold: salt. Slaves worked the salt pans. Small houses were built for the slaves to live in. When they were emancipated, the freemen continued to work. These small Dutch-designed houses exist today.

Can you imagine pink seawater? It is not bright blue but pink because of the high level of sea salt.

"C" Stands for Curacao

Sailors on a long voyage from Europe were afflicted with a terrible condition known as scurvy. Sick sailors were abandoned on the island of Curacao. When the ship returned, these sailors were healthy from eating fruits that had vitamin C. The name means "the island of healing."

Curacao was also one of the centers of the Slave Trade Triangle. Ships from Europe carried weapons and other goods to the coast of Africa. We were told that coastal Africans would go inland and capture people from tribes to sell as slaves. These captured people were shipped to the Caribbean and traded for tobacco, cocoa, and sugar. The raw materials were then shipped back to Europe for processing.

All three islands have had a tainted history, but today, they are thriving.

SMART TIP: Caution must be taken when visiting these islands. Remember, their laws and rules are different, and you do not want to have problems through ignorance. Investigate the laws and rules of a country before you visit.

NORWAY: Land of Firsts

By Natalie

Norway is a land of firsts. We take a ski lift to the top at Lillehammer, where the 1994 Winter Olympics was held, and stand at the gate of the ski jump, an experience that, again, people from Florida know little about. However, it is a motor coach ride through the narrow canyon that is the first that I will not forget.

After a two-hour cruise on the Sognefjord, we land in a small village called Gudvangen and hop on the motor coach. We travel along a road so narrow that no vehicle can pass.

My First Waterfall

"Oh, stop and pull over," we cry. "There is a waterfall." The bus empties to enable everyone to take a picture.

We move along the road, twisting and turning. "Oh stop, there is another waterfall with two crossing the other," the bus empties, except for the leader. His attitude is "You ain't seen nothing yet." And he is right; at every twist and turn, we see a new waterfall. Finally, the bus only half-empties.

My First Encounter with Sheep on the Road

As we continue down the narrow road, we suddenly stop. A flock of sheep is on the road, and they are not moving. The driver jumps out and waves his arms. The sheep only run around, but not off the road. The director follows and shouts at the sheep, but the stubborn sheep stay on the road. Finally, the director determines which one is the leader and shoos him to the ravine, and all the others follow.

My First Snowball Fight and Snow Angel

Oh, snow. We are at a high elevation. Being from Florida, the white fluffy stuff is new to me. I had seen pictures of kids snowball fighting, and I instigate one. This Floridian fares well in the snowball fight against the experienced ones who live in snow. I cannot understand why they were not as excited as I am about the brawl. Then, I get brazen. My joy trip ends when I hit the director squarely in the face. He is a good sport and laughs it off.

I remember seeing pictures of people making snow angels. Some of the others demonstrate for me. So I lie down in the snow on my back, face up, and make sweeping motions with my arms and legs. I understand that making snow angels is a real treat for those children who experience the first snow of the season.

An Encounter with Death

The canyon called Naerodal is narrow and winding; just plain scary. As we are going up, a car is coming down. We both stop. Looking down to the side was like looking into the depths of hell. There are no rails. The people on the bus gasp. There is some code of conduct for such a problem, and our driver has to back down. We are frightened as we look over the sides. We cheer when he makes it to a broader place in the road so the other car can pass.

We are heading back down to sea level. Now we know why the director said, "You ain't seen nothing yet." We see the granddaddy of all waterfalls—Tvinderfossen. It is widespread at the top and then separates into two, then appears to divide into four, and maybe divides again. It is not the tallest waterfall, but I must say it is the most unusual.

City of Bergen

After our "near-death" experience on the narrow roads, getting to Bergen and staying in a minimalist hotel is an experience. The tiny room has two small twin beds placed at a right triangle. One person can barely get into the bathroom to use a tiny toilet and brush their teeth in front of a tiny mirror.

There is an optional concert that night featuring the music of Norwegian composer Edvard Grieg. Mother goes to the concert, but the guide invites me to go with him to a local watering hole. When we get there, it looks like a rough group to me. We order a sandwich, and then suddenly, a man says something (in another language) to our guide. The guide jumps up and starts fighting this other man. I have no idea what it is about, but the owner not too graciously escorts us out (rather, kicks us out).

So, this trip to Norway had many firsts: magnificent falls, historical towns, my first snow angel, and the first and only time I had been kicked out of an establishment.

SMART TIP: As you venture into the Norwegian wilderness, remember: it's not just about fjords and waterfalls. Embrace the history and savor the experiences, but avoid getting on the wrong side of the locals.

USA: The Long Grey Line— Tales from West Point

By Evelyn

The fame of the Hudson River astounds us, and we are so curious as we take a river cruise up the "river that flows both ways." Although we pass many of the mansions along the river and famous sites like Sleepy Hollow, none are as exciting as the anticipation of seeing the United States Military Academy at West Point.

Sure, there are massive buildings, and the setting on the river is magnificent, but what fascinates me is the people who have been here over the years. The term "Long Grey Line" describes the cadets and graduates of West Point. The museum and its pictures of individuals in the Long Grey Line are enlightening. I especially appreciate focusing on the class of 1915, "the class the stars fell on." Of the 164 graduates, fifty-nine became generals, and this class went on to lead in the victory of World War II.

During 1941-1945, one cannot underestimate how these leaders and those in service were so significant in our eyes. Yes, I am a real patriot and try to keep up with events. During World War II, I was a child in the all-important years of 1941-1945; the heroes were my idols. One of the stars of this class of 1915 was Dwight D. Eisenhower, supreme commander in Europe and the thirty-fourth President of the United States. Another was Omar Bradley, a five-star general. I was in high school geometry class when we heard the song "Old

Soldiers Never Die —They Just Fade Away" and the speech of General Douglas MacArthur, who graduated in 1903. It would not be until many years later that I would understand his place in history.

The guide leads us to a greater understanding of life at West Point. She tells us how cadets are chosen, their daily lives, and their classes and options. But best of all, she tells stories that interest me.

An Unfinished Letter

As we make our way to the bluff overlooking the Hudson River, she relates anecdotes that underlie the academy's traditions. The spirit of the Long Grey Line is personified in the story of an unfinished letter. While cleaning the attic of an old building, some cadets found an old molded dusty box that contained some personal items of a former cadet. One was a letter written in the early twentieth century (remember the class of 1915). The letter to the cadet's sweetheart was never finished and never sent. It was a tearful letter expressing fears, dreams, and military life in general. Moved by the touching words, the cadets decided to finish the letter, adding their aspirations and experiences. The tradition continues with each graduating class adding thoughts to the unfinished letter.

A Chain Story

Spring of 1778: the British came, moving ships north of West Point to attack the Continental Army. How could we stop them? Their ships had to pass through a narrow bend in the Hudson River, which was at the bluff where we are standing. Each side knew that the Hudson River was the key to victory.

Answer: stretch a great chain across 500 yards from West Point to a large island (now called Continental Island). The chain weighed thirty-five tons and floated on rafts of fifty-foot white pine logs. Let the British try to get their big ships through here. The British failed.

We stand at West Point's Trophy Point, where thirteen links, a swivel, and clevis are seen. A plaque reads:

> THE GREAT CHAIN
> WAS ANCHORED
> NEAR THIS POINT
> 1778-1783

The Great Traitor

Knowing how vital control of the Hudson was, the British were interested in taking the complete fortress of West Point. Here comes a name that will forever live in infamy: Benedict Arnold. He thought the leaders of the Continental Army were neglecting him.

If the British Army gave him 20,000 pounds and rank of General, he would deliver the fortification plans of West Point to them. He failed to deliver. He went to England, where he died in 1801. Yet, in America, his name is synonymous with a traitor.

SMART TIP: Traveling in one's own country can reveal historical facts that have been forgotten. So, as you embark on your journey through the heartland, remember that travel is not just about the destination but the stories that unfold along the way.

EGYPT:
More than Pyramids

By Evelyn

Scarlet hibiscus and royal palms adorn the grounds of the Mena House. We are staying in one of the most prestigious hotels, which was once a hunting lodge for European royalty. We look out our balcony window and there it is: Cheops, the largest and tallest of the taupe-colored Great Pyramids.

"I can't believe that daddy climbed that pyramid," says Natalie.

She alludes to my husband Charles's stories about his 1953 archaeology trip to Egypt. His guide named Isa (Jesus), climbed the massive blocks with him. You may not realize how large these blocks are. Natalie stood in front of the bottom blocks and they were taller than her height. Natalie cannot follow in Daddy's footsteps. In 1976, the government stopped adventurers from climbing the pyramids.

One of our favorite places is the Luxor Temple, a grand complex on the banks of the Nile that welcomes you with towering statues of Rameses II, making every step feel like a journey back in time.

When asked about Egypt, the most common picture that comes to mind is one of the pyramids. But Egypt is more than pyramids; its history touches us in many ways.

Medo, Our Guide

Our guide for the odyssey is a learned Egyptologist named Mohammed. Because many of the males in Egypt have this name, he insisted we call him Medo.

We are given a bodyguard for our public excursions. Although it is initially unsettling, we soon become accustomed to the security.

We ask our guide about an attack that happened in June 1997, in the Valley of the Queens. Medo tells us that when he heard tat-tat-tat, "I knew immediately what it was. The death toll was 141 tourists, sixteen guides, and thirteen drivers. The terrorists hid in the mountains but were found. The publicity of these murders killed tourism for a least two years. Egypt has made many changes since then," he said.

Our trip occurred in 2006. Several other challenges to tourism have been endured since then, such as the Arab Spring and COVID-19. But Egypt continues to bounce back even better than before.

Medo guides us through the thousands of years of Egyptian dynasties and modern Egyptian history. One of our favorite places is the Cairo Museum, the Museum of Egyptian Antiquities.

In the Cairo Museum, we see the mask of Tutankhamun, or King Tut, the movie star of royalty. Perhaps one of the best reasons for his popularity is that the royal chambers in his tomb were hidden from plunderers. In 1922, Howard Carter found a dazzling array of treasures. A curse is supposed to follow anyone who goes into the tomb. The tomb itself was quite plain compared to the exquisite drawings on the tomb of Ramesses III.

Our adventures continue with a quick flight to Abu Simbel and then sailing on the Nile to the Valley of the Kings and Luxor (ancient Thebes). One of Natalie's favorite memories is playing ping-pong for hours on the boat sailing on the Nile—not every day does a good ping-pong player get beaten by an Egyptian boy on the Nile River.

SMART TIP: Egypt is one of the most exciting places to visit. Take an excursion up the Nile River, but be cognizant of current conditions. Check with your travel agent and the Department of State. Also, it is one of the hottest places in the summer. Always carry a bottle of water. Hydration is a must.

HUNGARY: Eternal Vigilance is the Price of Freedom

Budapest is a lively and thriving metropolis in Hungary. It is unique in that its name combines two cities: Buda, on the east, occupies a tall hill with a unique castle, and on the western side of the Danube River, Pest is the governmental part and other sites.

We have been to Budapest twice, and both times, we were amazed by its strength of character and the resolve of its people. We had read of Russian tanks destroying demonstrations for freedom and were shocked as the tanks rolled down their streets on our television screens. The desire of a people yearning to be free rang out in our minds.

Shoes Beside the Danube

We first encounter their suffering at a monument on the bank of the Danube River—bronzed shoes of people who had been in concentration camps. It was here that we are told about Memento Park. We hail a taxi for an experience which is not part of a regular tour.

Memento Park

The statue of Vladimir Lenin greets us with open arms. We stroll through the forty-one pieces from the Communist era of 1945-1989: Lenin, Marx, Engles, and Dimitrov.

Stalin's Boots

A twenty-six-foot bronze statue of Joseph Stalin once stood in central Budapest. When there were parades or holidays, the Communist leaders stood next to this statue, and the people had to cheer as they passed by. But on October 23, 1956, the crowd destroyed the statue to its knees. Stalin's boots were left and are now in Memento Park, a vivid reminder of this oppressor.

The theme of this park is not to honor these regimes but to remind people about what it is like to live under oppression. As the inscriptions remind us, the park is not about dictatorship; the park is about democracy. When the communists were in power, the people of Budapest had little opportunity to talk or think freely. With democracy, their minds and voices are free.

Stalin's boots statue at Memento Park is a powerful symbol of a dictator's fall. Preserving the boots captures the spirit of a people determined to walk away from tyranny and toward freedom.

Do You Want to Be a Spy?

Well, this is the film to see. The Communist regime produced films to provide training to secret police and other interested parties on how to defend the "law and order of the regime." You will learn from this film how to hide microphones and cameras, search houses, and recruit others to help. This unique presentation revealed the mindset of the Kadar regime (the Hungarian communist leader in Budapest).

Line Up for a Picture With Your New Car: the Trabant

This car—touted as better than a Mercedes—is tiny but has a great body of pressed fiber and plastics. Here is your beautiful blue-white dream car, a unique product of the German Democratic Republic. Test drive it—you will not forget the droning and clinking sound of the engine. It smells great, too—just like exhaust.

House of Terror

If Memento Park is not enough to learn about life under Communism, one must visit the House of Terror in Budapest. It was in these carpeted halls that decisions were made to designate Jews as their enemies and plan for their deportation.

We are escorted to the basement, where the AVH (secret police) tortured prisoners. It reminds us of the day we visited Dracula's Bran Castle and the torture chambers of the Middle Ages.

The places we visit in Budapest are there to remind people never to forget. They also help those who did not experience tyrannical regimes to remember that eternal vigilance is the price of freedom.

SMART TIP: Memento Park and the House of Terror are not on regular tours; ask a local tourist center for information.

PART 3

Love of Personal Growth

and Building Relationships

Navigating unfamiliar environments.
Getting away from provincial thinking.
Evaluating personal goals.
Experiencing spiritual awakening.

BOLIVIA:
Two Worlds

Travel seldom lets you interact and understand the country's people. We have that opportunity in Bolivia. Our guide in the capital LaPaz describes Bolivia's politics. Bolivia is made of diverse, multi-part systems in which native groups govern specific areas.

In LaPaz, we stay in the Hotel Europa, which has all the conveniences of home. In Santa Maria and Sucre, we stay in boutique hotels and we have little contact with the people. That is all about to change.

Bus Ride to Potosi

We travel to Potosi on a school bus. The three-hour bus ride is for native transportation (not tourists).

The older women, called cholitas, wear bowler hats with sweaters and red and yellow shawls, braided hair, long wide skirts, and layers of petticoats. The bowler hat was fashionable in the 1920s and was introduced to Bolivia by British railway workers. The hats were intended for the railway engineers, but when the hats arrived, they were too small, so they gave them to the native people. At

The vibrant and contrasting cultures of Bolivia are captured as this indigenous cholita, wearing a bowler hat, looks over LaPaz, a modern city.

one time, women wearing these clothes were socially ostracized and forbidden from public places and transport. However, since the 1960s, things have changed.

We smile at each of them, and they reciprocate with blackened teeth from years of chewing coca leaves.

Next comes a group of younger women with children and babies. They carry their little ones in front in large red, white, and green blankets twisted to make baby slings. The babies all have chullos, a knitted hat with earflaps made from alpaca or llama. The children are well-behaved.

Potosi: Nueva Terminal de Buses

We enter the bus terminal, which is one gigantic dome. Built in 2009, this vast terminal has everything, including vending machines, small stores selling things, and departures for all Bolivian cities. We are waiting for someone to pick us up, but we have no idea who it is. A gentleman who speaks English sees our distress and helps us find our driver.

It is a thirty-minute drive to our destination, as we desperately hold on to the car as the driver speeds around the mountain roads like a banshee.

Hotel Museo Cayara

We think this will be another boutique hotel—but it is not. It is a hacienda, the oldest in Bolivia and possibly on the continent, established in 1557. We will be experiencing the other side of Bolivia's population, which is different from that of the indigenous people.

We are greeted by friendly family members and enter a courtyard with pinkish-red terra cotta buildings and tile roofs. This hacienda was the home of colonial nobility, pioneers in silver and other mining, and government representatives. We have lunch in an area that is also a library. There are old notebooks by a family member who was a civil engineer and owned silver and limestone mines.

The town of Potosi retains its colonial feel. We drive by the famous Cero Rico Mountain, where silver has been mined for centuries. We see the Royal Mint, where Spanish coins were minted to return to Spain. The famous Street of Seven Turns protects locals from the chilly winds of the Altiplano.

Our introduction to the other side of Bolivia comes that night. The family has a large party for friends and invites us to join them. The group is made up of owners of local businesses and established families. Several of the people have lived extensively in the United States, and their families work in Washington D.C. in the Bolivian Embassy.

The history of this family of colonial nobility is displayed in the hacienda museum with paintings, furniture, and armory. There are eight rooms with objects of daily use, armor used in the conquest of Peru, muskets, sabers, and old rifles that go back to the War of Independence. This is not just a museum but the family's dear possessions.

The hacienda also includes two notable libraries, which are full of old books and documents of historical value.

SMART TIP: In our travel to Potosi, we failed to record the company's contact and identification of the driver. When arranging for transportation, be sure to secure the company's name and ask for the driver's ID.

PERU: Machu Picchu—Where the Happy Overcomes the Miserable

By Natalie

Machu Picchu means "old mountain" in Quechua. Molded by eons of wind and shaking the earth, the old mountains rise as a series of razor-sharp peaks and deep hollows.

An entire city built in the fifteenth century served as a center of worship, a place for astronomical observation, and a place of solemn escape for the royal Inca families. What kind of people lived and worked in this place?

We arrive in Cuzco, Peru, the capital of the Inca Empire, and traveling by train, we look down at the deep valley cut by the Urubamba River. Condors and other birds are floating on the mountain currents.

We pass the famous agricultural terraces on the steep hillside as we ride along. Terraces wrap around the hillside like concentric circles of braids. The significant benefits are soil conservation and protection from erosion. People haul rich topsoil from the lower lands. Farmers still work on these lands just as they have done for centuries.

My Peace Shaken

And then my peaceful thoughts are interrupted. One of the ladies in our group is a constant complainer. This person has all the designer clothes, a fabulous handbag, and showy jewelry with a pedicure to match. She appears to have everything, but her misery is evident.

As we ride by a farm, we see a farmer hoeing his crop with his two young children—perhaps ages six and seven. They have their little hoes and the entire family is talking and laughing in the field. As children are wont to do, the kids horse around; sometimes they engage in a sod fight—even throwing at the dad—who also laughs. Eventually, they all return to work.

I overhear the lady who has everything say, "Look at those children. It is so terrible they are so poor. They should not have to do all that work."

She continues to talk about these "poor, little peasants."

I am shattered. Here is a person who appears to have everything and cannot see the happiness of other people who may not have all the "things" that she has. I determine to avoid this person.

Back to the Top of Machu Picchu

We get off the train and are pointed to the path to the top of the mountain. We slough our way through grounds that nature has taken mainly back. We are indeed forging a deep relationship with the earth and the community of explorers who have gone before. Ascending to the summit is an "on top of the world" feeling.

Inca Ruins at Pisac

One of the best-known Inca ruins is at Pisac and consists of four groups: the Temple of the Sun, baths, water fountains, and a ceremonial platform. It also has a large marketplace. Walking to the market, we meet another working boy, Eddie. We are looking for a specific tapestry, and I ask Eddie for help. Eddie is about ten and can speak English well. He helps us navigate this huge marketplace to find water, drinks, food, and washrooms. He hears me say that I want a tapestry or wall hanging with the sun god, and he knows right where to go. He leads us to his mother's table of beautiful blankets, and we buy the tapestry we have been searching for.

One of the natives tells us Eddie is slow. When we get ready to leave, Eddie comes on the bus to say goodbye and shows us a small clay whistle he is selling. Everyone on the bus buys one; I still have mine. We will always remember Eddie, who could outdo any of the elite sales and marketers we know. He should write a book titled *How to Sell to Suckers*.

Machu Picchu is more than just the best-traveled tourist destination. It is an experience of people as well as places. Etched in my mind are the farmer and his happy children and Eddie, who admirably outsmarted all of us.

This slice of life in a few moments taught me how travel can teach tolerance and cultural understanding and how other people at other times are just as intelligent and capable as those of us in a "sophisticated world." For amidst the rugged beauty of the Andes lies a wealth of wisdom waiting to be discovered—one smile and one interaction at a time.

Eddie, the whistle wizard, outshines the elite marketers of the world—one clay whistle at a time. Machu Picchu may be unforgettable, but it's Eddie, the master salesman, who truly stole the show and our hearts.

SMART TIP: Take the time to smile at the workers you encounter along your travels; their resilience and joy in adversity will inspire and uplift you in ways you never imagined possible.

RUSSIA: Peasants' Road to Moscow

We have the privilege that only a few tourists experience while traveling overland by bus to Moscow. We pick up the official Russian guide at the border. This no-nonsense gal speaks English very well but has forgotten how to smile. She rules these American tourists with an iron fist. We don't think she likes us very much.

On this trip, we see two major cities, but most of the way, we travel on desolate highways and through small rural villages. We are on the peasants' tour, and a part of Russia that is not shown or written about.

Saint Petersburg

Most tourists who visit Russia are on a cruise ship that docks in Saint Petersburg. Peter the Great built this magnificent city in the eighteenth century. Visitors enjoy ornate buildings such as the Winter Palace, the Hermitage, and other museums.

On the Peasants' Road

The road to Moscow from Saint Petersburg winds through 393 miles of villages and farms. Abandoned German tanks are left along the road to remind the Russian people of their World War II victory. Babushkas (older women) sell mushrooms gathered from the adjoining forests. These Russian peasants are famous for their wild dinners and use all types of plants from the woods to make these meals.

We pass through Oryol, a small city on the Oka River. Standing in the center of town is a towering figure atop a horse in full imperial regalia, sword in one hand, cross in the other. This statue is Russia's first czar, Ivan the Great—better known as the Terrible (1547-1584).

Moscow

The Russian guide arranges our visit to Red Square at sunset. It is lighted in brilliant colors, emphasizing stately buildings and onion-domed cathedrals. If her goal is to impress us with the greatness of Red Square, she accomplishes it. We are overwhelmed.

We visit a grocery store to discover local traditions. The store shelves are limited to one product each—such as canned peas, beans, soap, and toilet paper.

Red Square's iconic onion domes of St. Basil's Cathedral stand in striking contrast to Russia's rural landscapes and villages on the peasant's road.

Bush Bathrooms and Brown Wiggly Things

We return to our peasants' road with no gas stations or restaurants. Our guide says, "Our next stop will be the bush bathrooms."

We pull off the road in a large opening. "Just follow the path," she instructs us. We trek along a dirt trail, expecting to find a small building behind the large bushes. Along the path, streamers of tissue dangle from bushes and shrubs. We still expect just any type of hut, but there is nothing but toilet tissue adorning the trees. These are the "bush bathrooms." It is not the place for spoiled American tourists, so we bite the bullet and high-tail it out of there. We do note that one could wash hands in a bucket nailed to a tree and dry with a communal towel.

Our overnight stop is at Smolensk, a city in the Western steppes of Russia. That night, our place of abode is a Russian truck stop. After a meal of rubber chicken, boiled potatoes, and borscht, the bus driver asks Natalie if she would like to stay for a dance. It would be a grand opportunity to "rub shoulders with the locals." She graciously declines.

The tiny motel room is on the first floor—no air conditioning and no screens, but an abundance of bugs and mosquitoes. Evelyn decides to take a bath in the tub (there is no shower) and she runs the water. The water color is green with little brown wiggly bugs doing the backstroke. Evelyn skips the bath.

We are at the end of our Russian peasants' road and kiss our charming Russian escort goodbye. We tip her for keeping us safe and taking good care of us.

SMART TIP: Although we learned about Russian culture, we also learned much about ourselves. We proudly stand and sing the "Star Spangled Banner" at every ball game or event. If someone looks at us, we smile and say, "We have been to Russia."

SOUTH AFRICA: Where the Compass Needles Go Haywire

The biting August winter wind stings our faces as we read, "You are now at the southernmost tip of the continent of Africa." We drove over the scenic route from Cape Town, passing by the towering cliffs that drop like lead into the sea. The Portuguese sailors call this Cape Agulhas, meaning "Cape of Needles." Their compass needles do not work because of the earth's magnetism; the only direction is directly north. Here is where the warm waters of the Indian Ocean meet the cold waters of the Atlantic. As rough as it is, we wonder how any ships could navigate around here. Many did not.

Only three days earlier, we had left steamy Florida to fly into Cape Town for a fourteen-day jaunt through South Africa. We had endured questions like, "Why do you want to go there?"

Although we have been to eighty-eight countries, this trip was filled with the most surprises, not only of beauty and culture but also with enlightened history lessons to help us understand Africa and the world.

Our home for the night, the fishing village of Arniston, has gleaming white Dutch cottages and brown-thatched roofs. The Arniston was a British ship that wrecked in 1815, killing 378 passengers. In the hotel, a map with fifty-six pins marks wrecks in these turbulent waters. We have read about the Cape of Good Hope in geography books but had no idea of its turbulence and hidden dangers.

About seven miles out in these waters lies a lonely, desolate expanse of flat rocks named Robben Island, which means "Island of the

Seals." In 1636, the Dutch found this foreboding place ideal for their undesirables and began to bring criminals of all sorts. No prisoner would dare escape in these turbulent waters. In the mid-nineteenth century, the British found it was a great place to isolate lepers and political prisoners. It is said that the guards met the new arrivals and said to them: "This is the island. Here you will die."

In 1963, the South African government sentenced Nelson Mandela and other political activists to the island for life. Mandela was teaching about the inequities of the apartheid system and was accused of treason. He remained there until 1982, when, after being treated for tuberculosis, he was sent to another maximum-security prison. When free elections were held in 1994, he was released and became the first president of the New South Africa.

On this rocky island, we see a small, barren cell with a bucket for a toilet. Mandela lived here for nearly twenty years. What did prisoners do? According to the guide, Mandela and other prisoners were condemned to hard labor, which consisted of breaking stones from the quarry. He could have one visitor for thirty minutes each year. He could write and receive one letter every six months. His letters to Winnie, his wife, are quite poignant. He proclaims his love for her and apologizes that his stands have landed him in prison, but that it must be. He refers to these as dark years and describes the harsh daily routine in his letters. However, these years were the crucible for transformation. His intelligence and dignified defiance eventually bent the most brutal prison authorities to his will. For his work, Nelson Mandela won the Nobel Peace Prize in 1993.

SMART TIP: When traveling to South Africa, respect the country's rich tapestry of cultures, languages, and traditions. Additionally, educate yourself on the country's complex history, including apartheid and its aftermath, to better understand contemporary South Africa.

FRANCE:
Under the Eiffel Tower

In 1889, the Eiffel Tower was built for the World's Fair. At the time, artists and writers criticized it as ugly and degrading. The famous writer Guy de Maupassant hated the tower so much that he frequently ate lunch under it because it was the only place in Paris where you could not see it.

The intent had been to tear it down after the fair, but Parisians were proud that French ingenuity and know-how had built the world's tallest building (and it remained so until the Empire State Building in New York knocked it off its perch.)

But now, for over 130 years, this place of a million pictures (or more) has been the distinctive symbol of Paris. Almost everyone who visits the area has a miniature Eiffel Tower among their souvenirs. A visit to Paris is incomplete without a visit to the tower to get their picture to post on social media. We are about to get one of those social media photos ourselves!

So here we are, ready to revisit the tower. It is even more exciting than the first. With great expectations, we talk about how we want to climb to the top.

As we approach the Eiffel Tower, a storm is looming. It rapidly gets darker. As we get off the bus and head for the tower, the storm's full force arrives, and we run under the tower for cover. All the other tourists are huddled around with us.

We hunker low together under the tower. Water rushes under our feet, and my lightweight, white windbreaker whips in the strong breeze. My hair may be standing on end. I know what that means: electricity is near. More tourists with hunched shoulders holding bags or papers over their heads crowd into where we are huddled. Natalie and I try to move from the edge to the middle, hoping not to be toppled over by the wind.

This monster thunderstorm arrived unannounced. The black demon descends, devouring what had been a lovely August day. It is ruthless—breathing fire and intent on destruction. We are in its path and will all die in this iron electric chamber.

Boom!

Blinding light.

Crack!

A bolt of lightning bobs toward the horizon.

Boom!

The smell of ozone, angry water, and frightened tourists screams.

And as suddenly as the monster appeared, it fled. The storm stopped as abruptly as it came.

We had been under a great iron structure lighting rod, standing in a puddle of attractive medium. This crowd of strangers looked at each other, sighing, and remembered again that we are tourists—risk-takers leaving the comfort zones of our homes to travel the world.

Natalie and I return to normal with plans to climb the stairs to the second floor. Others eventually return to take in the sites of Versailles, rejoice in the Arc de Triumph, and have their pictures made. Yes, we brushed our hair, took off our wet jackets, hid our wet feet, and snapped the picture for social media.

Here we are, standing in front of the Eiffel Tower.

SMART TIP: Be prepared when traveling. Unexpected events, like sudden thunderstorms, can disrupt your plans. Always bring a light rain-repellent jacket and a small umbrella.

FRANCE:
In Love and War

Did you know that Valentine's Day has a strong association with France? During the Middle Ages, the popular belief was that birds began to mate halfway through the second month of the year. Because of these lovebirds, lovers began to see the day as special and exchanged love notes and tokens on Valentine's Day.

We are on a river trip, moving lazily up the Seine River, and encounter lots of love and wars. On French soil, the Vikings, the Hundred Years War, the Franco-Prussian War, World War I, and World War II all sought to conquer this land of love.

Choose One Soldier

While we are on the ship, our director, Paul, tells us that this will be one of the most challenging days we have experienced. We are going to Normandy, Omaha Beach, and the American Cemetery. And then Paul says, "I did something you might like to try. When you are at the cemetery, choose one soldier from your state. I chose Private Dick Sandler from Minnesota. When I got home, I researched and found his family. I wrote to them and visited them. I wanted the family to know their loved one was not forgotten even after these many years."

"What a great gesture!" we say.

We travel to the beach where the invasion occurred. It was called Operation Overlord—D-Day, June 6, 1944. Participating countries occupied five different beaches. The US forces landed at Omaha Beach.

How Did They Do It?

"Impossible!" we say.

How could soldiers climb these walls? These cliffs are straight up. They landed on a sandy beach, and all the while, Germans were fortified in bunkers shooting down at them. We enter one of the bunkers on top of the cliff. It has two-feet-thick concrete walls reinforced with steel beams; double timbers were also used to strengthen it. We look at the view of the beach from inside the bunker. These bunkers were so strongly built that exploding bombs and mortars from the outside could not destroy them. The only way was for someone to get close enough to throw a hand grenade into the small open space used as a lookout or a gun port.

We walk across a wide field to the Normandy American Cemetery and Memorial. It is a semi-circular building with a twenty-two-foot statue called the Spirit of American Youth. An astonishing 9,386 American war dead are buried in this part of the cemetery. Also, there were 307 unknowns, and 14,000 heroes were returned to their families and next of kin. We gather for a ceremony ending with "Battle Hymn of the Republic." Each person is given a red rose to place by a grave.

And then we are there; speechless, overwhelmed. The crosses are arranged in organized rows as far as the eye can see. So Natalie and I begin scouting for soldiers from Florida. We scour several rows; the soldiers are from everywhere. Finally, we did settle on one.

A rose for a fallen hero: Honoring a young man at Normandy Cemetery. The quiet tribute amidst rows of white crosses makes this site unforgettable.

The private was probably only eighteen or nineteen; some mother's little boy caught up in the throngs of a horrible war. He had probably received and sent valentines of love to his "sweetie." He had survived D-day and made it inland for the liberation of France. So many thoughts: what would his life have been like if he had lived? Why were these boys in front of us killed while others survived to remember them?

We Leave a Rose on his Grave

There is a group that does not believe in dark tourism—tourists going to places where terrible things happen. We do not call it dark, but rather, "enlightened tourism." We do care. As we write this, we wipe a few tears from our eyes.

SMART TIP: Visiting such memorials can be an exercise in spiritual awakening and evaluating our goals and lives.

FRANCE:
We're Not in Kansas Anymore

Pat Nevard and Grant Kelly,
as told to Evelyn

The great cities of France, such as Paris, Lyon, and Marseilles, are marvelous and commanding. But did you realize that most of France is rural, with farmland and small villages?

If you want to travel between cities like Paris and Nice, you can travel by high-speed train, drive down a highway, or take two scenic highways through rural areas.

Pat and Grant are seasoned travelers. Their adventures include tours to the South Pacific and many places in Europe. They decide to drive from Paris to Nice. According to their research, it will take a little over nine hours. In addition to seeing the lavender-studded Provence, they will go through several friendly towns like Toulouse, but the main attraction for them is seeing the Mediterranean and the French Riviera.

Their travels are always well-planned and systematic. They have chosen to go to France and see the countryside. Therefore, renting a car is the best way for them to see the cities and countryside.

Pat and Grant rent a car and carefully read France's laws and road rules. They even learn conversational phrases in French. With such meticulous planning, nothing can go wrong . . . or can it?

Driving through the French countryside from Paris to Nice is beautiful; they are enjoying it.

The fuel is low, so they stop for gas (or petrol, as it is known in Europe). Grant inserts his credit card at the pump and the car is filled with gas; no problem. He takes the card out of the pump and drives off.

Looking through the back window, they see a man hanging out of a car window, screaming and waving furiously. At the same time, a police car rushes behind them, flashing its lights. They stop. The angry man in the first car gets out and starts yelling in French. They have no idea what is happening. Then the policeman gets out of his car. Fortunately, he speaks some English.

"You left the station without paying," he said, trying to calm the other man, who was the station owner.

"Oh, but I paid by the card. The gas started running," explained Grant.

"Do you have a receipt?" asked the policeman.

"No, I never bother with receipts."

"You were supposed to go into the station to pay for gas. You left without paying," explained the officer.

Grant stated, "In the States, when you insert your card, it unlocks, and you can pump the gas."

"This is France, not the United States. You should have known to go into the store and pay," said the agitated policeman.

The store owner is screaming in French all the time.

The policeman calms the situation and asks how much he owes.

The owner writes on the back, dusty window, "40 euros."

Grant pays it and leaves.

While driving down the road, both are visibly shaken.

Pat says, "That was scary. Do you realize we could have been arrested?"

When Pat talks about this trip, does she talk about the lavender-studded Provence and the balmy Mediterranean? NO. She tells the scary story of nearly getting arrested in France.

SMART TIP: Driving in a foreign country is unlike at home. Know the country's laws and rules of the road, how to drive on their side of the road, and save all receipts—whether they are convenient or not.

INDIA: Culture Shock and the Land of Extremes

There are people everywhere, scooters buzzing, cows walking up to you, snake charmers, Bollywood, temples, palaces, and the smell of garlic and spices. The culture in India is the most diverse of any we have experienced—but also the most exciting. This is why the tapestry of India is so fascinating and mysterious.

We arrive in Mumbai, formerly known as Bombay. It was 2:00 a.m., and we hailed a cab to take us to Hotel Taj. The streets are lined with cars with people sleeping on top of them. The streets are packed with people like it is the middle of the day. People are hitting our cab to get our attention and asking us to give them money. As we ride along, I can feel tears in my eyes. Had we made a mistake in coming to India? When we get to Hotel Taj, Natalie confides that she has the same feelings. (This hotel would later be the object of a terrible terrorist attack and the theme of the movie called *Hotel Mumbai*.)

The next day, we finally meet our private guide and driver. He leads us on a tour of Mumbai's "touristy" places, such as the waterfront and the Jain temple. However, the outdoor laundry is one of the most unusual "touristy" places. We stand above and overlook Dhobi Ghat, the world's largest laundry. For eighteen to twenty hours each day, over 7,000 people flog, scrub, dye, and bleach clothes on concrete pens, hang them on ropes, and neatly press them to deliver to customers.

We are unsettled again as we are dropped off at the airport to fly to Udaipur. This is where we meet our guide, Shailesh, who will become our lifelong friend. He will be with us the rest of the way. The tears have abated, and we relax to enjoy this exotic country. Shailesh takes us first to a night market and becomes the guardian of these two blondes. If anyone appears to come up to sell us anything, he immediately gets in between us, and they get the message and back off. Shailesh takes good care of us and is an exceptional guide.

Cultural Differences

Having a personal driver and guide is very important to grasp cultural differences fully. We travel from place to place by car. Since the British were in India, they drive on the left side of the road. Our driver does not speak English but knows how to speak with the horn. All drivers in India blow horns constantly; there are few lights and stop signs. Cities are very noisy places.

The ancient cities of India are fascinating. In Udaipur, we take a boat to our hotel, which is built in the middle of a lake. Then, we are taken to a master seamster, where we are fitted for a silk coat. We travel to unique cities full of color: Jodhpur, where houses are painted blue, and Jaipur, where most buildings are painted pink.

The people of India are very kind and curious. A lady approaches Natalie to touch and smell her skin and hair. Shailesh explains that women are curious because they do not see many people with fair skin, blonde hair, and blue eyes.

Best Way to Bypass Traffic

The highways are even more interesting. Buses are packed inside with people sitting on top and hanging onto the back and windows. We pass cows, camels, and people walking on the side of the road. Indian women are the delivery trucks; they pick up a load of rocks and carry them to the paving area in their skirts.

While heading for Agra, we are stuck in traffic because of an accident. It is a major highway. Instead of waiting for the wreck to clear, the driver takes off across the median and drives on the other side against traffic. We keep our heads between our legs, refusing to look. We make it. Imagine doing this on major interstates in the US.

We think about India often. This trip to India, the country of extremes, helped us realize how important it is to understand cultural differences. It is marvelous to see the great historic sites, visit magnificent palaces, and ride an elephant, but having the personal touch lets you see how people need to understand each other.

An Elephant Ride to Amber Fort: Evelyn and Natalie embrace India's exotic charm and cultural splendor.

SMART TIP: Forge friendships with your guides. Not only will they help you navigate the intricacies of the culture, but they may also become lifelong friends, enriching your journey in ways you could have never imagined.

AUSTRIA, USA, Michigan: A Tale of Two Chapels "Silent Night"

1818 It was the best of times; it was the worst of times. It was wonderful for Father Josef Mohr in the village of Oberndorf, Austria because Christmas was coming and the war with Napoleon was over. It was the worst of times because a mouse had chewed the organ's inner mechanisms, and there could be no church music. The war had ravaged the village, leaving turmoil, suffering, and hunger. Needed was the spirit of Christmas and joyful music to provide hope.

Sitting on a small hill in the peaceful Alps, he pondered his situation of having no music. Inspired, he took a pen and wrote a poem, "Stille Nacht, Heilige Nacht." Why not set the poem to music? He contacted his organist, Franz Gruber, who composed a melody using his guitar. The church had Christmas music, and we have the best-known Christmas hymn: "Silent Night."

Chapel One: Oberndorf, Austria

During an excursion from nearby Salzburg, we are dropped off in the village of Oberndorf. The whole city is saturated with memorabilia and souvenirs of "Silent Night." We go through the hoopla and climb the steps to a small white octagonal building with a tiled roof, a cupola bell helmet, and a lantern.

River flooding destroyed the first little chapel, but in 1936, a new chapel on a higher site was built. The whole town of Oberndorf moved about a half mile upstream. What a joy to experience the site commemorating where the great Christmas carol was written and performed.

Chapel Two: Frankenmuth, Michigan

I am in Frankenmuth, Michigan, and pass by a fifty-six-foot-tall chapel on the southern tip of Bronner's Christmas Wonderland. Billboards on the interstate advertised this wonderland; but seeing the little Silent Night chapel is a wonder in itself.

In 1976, Wally Bronner was on a European trip buying ornaments and memorabilia for his Christmas store. The family had started the Christmas store in 1945, the same year the war ended. When visiting Oberndorf, he had a marvelous idea: to build a replica of this chapel at Bronner's Christmas Wonderland. He got permission from the Oberndorf city officials and set out to create the replica in Frankenmuth at the south end of town.

Care was taken to make it as authentic as possible. Inside, guests may hear the message of Christ's birth, as told in Luke 2:1-19, in thirty different languages. Outside lamp posts line the walkway with Silent Night displayed in 300 languages. "Silent Night" may be heard inside and outside the chapel grounds. Bronner's display also includes a life-size nativity scene. The inspirational landmark is fully illuminated at night and is open daily for visitation and meditation at no charge.

From Austria to Michigan, the story of "Silent Night" has an important message for today's world.

SMART TIP: Traveling to places like these two chapels isn't just about exploring history—it's about deepening your appreciation for peace, love, and harmony that transcends borders and languages. Take the opportunity to reflect on the message of "Silent Night" and its relevance in today's world.

LITHUANIA: Hill of Crosses—Was It the Devil Who Made Me Do It?

By Natalie

Did you ever dream of seeing a genuine miracle? An area in Lithuania will fulfill that dream.

We are traveling in the Baltic States in an area many tourists and historians neglect. Vilnius, the capital of Lithuania, was once a powerhouse in Europe. The union believed in ethnic diversity, religious tolerance, and parliamentary rule. However, the great powers of Russia, Austria-Hungary, and the German Empires desired this commonwealth's marvelous land and wealth. Devastated by two World Wars, they became part of the Soviet Union.

The Miracle Begins

Russia conquered Lithuania and made it part of the Russian Empire in 1795. The people were not enthralled with being a part of Russia but were unsuccessful in their rebellions in 1831 and 1863. Many of their people were killed, and families could not locate the bodies of their loved ones. So they found an area that had once been a fort and put up crosses in their remembrance. Over generations, people added crosses, crucifixes, statues of the Virgin Mary, and carvings of Lithuanian patriots. It had become a tribute to not only remembering family, but also remembering the endurance of people despite threats.

In 1900, there were 130 crosses. In 1938, there were over 400. This is the Hill of Crosses.

Soviet Suppression of Religion

Under the Soviets from 1944-1990, the people were victims of religious persecution, and there was a prohibition of religious teachings. But remember, they had a great tradition of religious freedom, and these beliefs were passed down through their families. They desired to safeguard these freedoms, which meant safeguarding the Hill of Crosses. Even under threats, they carried crosses to commemorate loved ones and pray for health or success. The hill became a symbol of resistance to Soviet suppression.

Here Come the Bulldozers

The Soviet government brought in the bulldozers and knocked over the crosses. In 1961, they demolished over 5,000 crosses. Overnight, more crosses would appear. How did they do it? The KGB was puzzled; they monitored all accesses to the hill. Somehow, the crosses kept building up. In 1975, they bulldozed 1,200 more crosses—and new ones still kept appearing. Three times, the bulldozers came, and the same thing happened. They even threatened to flood the area if this did not stop. But the crosses kept coming.

Soviet-Era Ends

When the Soviets left, there were 14,387 big and 41,000 small crosses. The Hill of Crosses is a pilgrimage site. Each pilgrim to the area tries to leave a cross or rosary. They can make one from branches, pebbles, or even grass if they do not already have one. Each year, new crosses appear—there are perhaps 200,000 to 300,000 now.

We saw the Hill of Crosses as part of a Baltic trip in 1996. The guide said we could leave a cross as we entered the site. There was a kiosk of crosses where we could purchase crosses to leave. More importantly, he stressed that you should not take a cross as a souvenir, for if you do, you will have seven years of bad luck.

Crossing the Path of the Devil?

I explore independently, trekking through narrow paths of thousands of crosses. I step on an object that piques my curiosity. I dig up the object, and it is a plastic silver-colored cross with a word written in Russian on the back. As I clean the dirt off the cross, a man asks me if I want it. He tells me I could take the cross. I say, "No, thank you," and explain the seven-year curse.

He tells me that he works at the site and that they encourage visitors to take a cross. Being young and naive, I believe the man and keep the cross. As we pull away from the site on the bus, I show our guide and tell him about the worker who encouraged me to take the souvenir. With wide eyes open, he says no such worker was at the site.

Was it the devil who made me do it?

The next seven years were very difficult for me. I still have that plastic cross and will return it to the Hill of Crosses someday when I return to Lithuania.

The Hill of Crosses: A testament to faith and resilience. Thousands of crosses are powerful symbols of unwavering devotion, surviving destruction to rise again in spiritual defiance.

SMART TIP: Never take something you did not purchase or belongs to that country, even if it is offered to you. Picking up rocks or other souvenirs is illegal in most countries, especially from archeological dig sites.

DENMARK: Hans Christian Andersen and The Ugly Duckling

Imagination is a thing of beauty. We are in Odense, Denmark, at the home of Hans Christian Andersen. "The Ugly Duckling" comes alive as we venture into this fabulous writer's creative mind.

Odense, Denmark, is a picturesque town that looks like someone has thrown colored Monopoly pieces down and landed on the cobblestone streets. It is the third largest city in the country and about one hundred miles from Copenhagen.

We probably all have read some of the stories that Hans Christian Andersen wrote: "The Ugly Duckling," "The Little Mermaid," "Emperor's New Clothes," or maybe "The Princess and the Pea." It is such an honor to be where he was born in 1805 and where he is recognized as one of Denmark's greatest citizens.

From the ages of two to fourteen, he lived in the little yellow, half-timbered house near the Odense Cathedral. Touring the little house, we see very humble rooms and the poverty that marked his early years. His mother was an illiterate washerwoman, and his father was a shoemaker who delighted in telling his son stories. The stories of the "Arabian Nights" especially piqued his imagination.

Our favorite story is "The Ugly Duckling," about a young duck who was laughed at and excluded from the other ducklings. Even his mother did not like him. But then something unique happened; the ugly duckling became a large, white, gorgeous creature—a swan. This story parallels Andersen's experience. He went to Copenhagen hoping to become an actor. He was laughed at for being too skinny and uneducated to enter the theatre. But the mid-1800s were a time of the Romantics in literature and a time of Danish nationalism. Hans started writing stories from his youth with a majestic imagination, and they soon became a hit. The "human" ugly duckling became a beautiful swan. His 156 stories have been recognized internationally and written into plays and movies.

Hans did not fit in with Copenhagen's high society. His behavior and upbringing were not considered to be proper for elite society. It is said that once, after returning from a speaking tour, he heard someone say that, "Now our world-famous orangutan is home again."

His simplicity is also shown in his home. There is not much there except Ikea-like furniture, a bookstore, and a souvenir shop. We buy a statue of the Little Mermaid and his biography.

Evelyn was there again in 2015, and plans were in the works for an H.C. Andersen museum like no other. It opened in 2021. Drawn from the plans of the Japanese architect Kengo Kama, the museum has the usual round buildings, soft curves, and a magical garden. The guide says, "You end up somewhere between what is outside and inside." High hedges guide you through a dense, dark green garden with crooked fir trees, and then suddenly, you are in the light garden with fanciful flowers. These hedges form the walls from different scenes that encourage our imagination.

Spaces underground tell fairy tale stories and help urge one's imagination along by appealing to all the senses. For example, the little mermaid will be under the floor, and those on top will feel like they are underwater. State-of-the-art technologies interact with the world around them.

It is hard for me to describe such an experience—as designed by the architects and creators—but it had to be different to honor Hans Christian Andersen's imagination.

The Little Mermaid in Copenhagen

Sculptor Edvard Eriksen created a statue of The Little Mermaid on a rock in Copenhagen harbor. Unveiled in 1913, it has been a significant tourist attraction ever since.

SMART TIP: Danes are very proud of their nationality. Their flag, the Dannebrogen, is the oldest national flag in the world and is found at homes, dinner parties, restaurants, and airports.

INDIA:
Taj Mahal—A True Love Story

The Taj Mahal is one of the most recognizable buildings and the world's most iconic monument. It is featured on textbooks, book covers, calendars, and framed pictures. But why was it built?

"A teardrop on the cheek of time," Rabindranath Tagore, a beloved Indian poet, called the Taj Mahal. Many tears have been shed in building this structure, viewing it in pictures, or experiencing it in person. But considering the love story behind it, it becomes even more meaningful.

Agra, India

Mumtaz, a beautiful Persian aristocrat, was selling silks and beads. She was charming, well-educated, and cultured; also, she was versed in Arabic and Persian, and was known as an accomplished poet. While seeing her in the bizarre, Shah Jahan was smitten with her. Through deals with her father, she had been betrothed to the Shah when she was fourteen and he was fifteen, but it would be five years before their marriage. In India's complex world of politics, having solid and supportive allies was essential.

But the marriage of Mumtaz and Jahan was not just a political alliance. They had a loving, caring marriage. She was frequently pregnant but traveled with him throughout his earlier military campaigns, and even joined him in a rebellion against his father. She was his adviser and confidant, as well as his constant companion. They were married for nineteen years and had eight sons and six daughters.

In 1629, Jahan defeated his half-brother and became the emperor. Mumtaz became First Lady or Queen of the Great. She had enormous political power. It is said that she often intervened on behalf of the poor; she also patronized several poets and scholars. Sitting on the council, she was hidden behind a curtain. She placed her hand on his back if she did not agree with something. From her counsel, he would forgive an accused or commit to death.

However, her reign as queen was short—only three years. While giving birth to her fourteenth child, after a prolonged labor of thirty hours, she died. Shah Jahan was devastated. He did not appear in public for a year, and when he finally appeared, his hair was white, his face was worn, and his back was bent.

Mumtaz's body had been temporarily interred, but Shah commissioned a mausoleum for his undying love and marital devotion. This building was to have striking symmetry, dazzling white marble, an impressive scale, and glistening jewels.

It took years to build, and the details still astound anyone who lays eyes upon it, but the love story is more remarkable. Rumors are that he killed the architect and designers who worked on the Taj Mahal so they could never build something as significant.

The Taj Mahal: An enchanting vision of serenity and romance. This timeless monument reflects an epic love story that continues to inspire awe.

When you go to the Taj, you can feel that it is not just a building but a passion of a man's love for his wife. You can feel this undying devotion through the years when you look at the ivory-white columns, the lacy combinations of Persian Ottoman and Islamic art, and the symmetry and harmony throughout this architectural masterpiece. The long, picturesque pool reflects love and devotion. The care for something so sacred as love even shows in the manicured grounds.

SMART TIP: Evelyn purchased a ten-inch marble tile decorated with blue flowers and jewels that replicate the design of the Taj Mahal. When buying souvenirs, purchase products that are made in and that represent the country, city, or site.

JAPAN:
From Okinawa with Love

Kiyoko (Kay) and little Margie with Evelyn.
(We include this story of someone who traveled from another country to the United States as an honor to war brides.)

March, 1945—Okinawa, Japan

The weather was pleasant in March. The bougainvillea, iris, hibiscus, and azalea give us bright red, purple, yellow, and pink flowers to admire. It was so pleasant and nice to be alive. Kiyoko, who had just turned fifteen on March 29, was happy with her family, but everything may not have been well.

Kiyoko Speaks

The American forces had taken the nearby Kerama Islands and we heard that they may be headed our way. We understood that they were terrible, and we could expect the most horrible things to happen to us. We did not despair or give up. It is not the Japanese way. We knew we had to be courageous and trust our superior forces to conquer that evil devil. We determined that we would save face and never surrender.

April 1, 1945—Okinawa, Japan

The Americans landed on the beach, and our best chances at survival were to split up. Mother went north with brother and sister; the Japanese military had already conscripted another brother, and his fate was never to be known. Father, another sister, and I went south. We did not know that we would be going directly into the fray.

Bam!

Rat-a-tat-tat—that is all we heard for days and days.

We crouched down, hiding every place we could. Fearing the worst for ourselves, we lived in terror. We ate potato leaves and drank sugar cane juice. When the bombing got more fierce, we hid in a cave, where our sister was killed and our father was injured and taken away, presumably to a hospital for treatment. I lived in terror, but the fighting became fainter and fainter; farther and farther away.

The last remnants of Japanese resistance made their stand on June 21. The bloody Battle of Okinawa was over, leaving untold dead on each side. I was taken to an internment camp after surrendering, but then I was released. I hitchhiked from the camp to find my mother, brother, and sister, which was a joyful reunion because we were presumed dead in the southern battleground.

We headed back home and found ruins, so we lived wherever we could find shelter. However, I was determined to complete high school, where I studied English and worked as a housemaid for a kind military family. I later got a job at the PX, the military store. I had such mixed feelings; I was sad and happy at the same time. We knew that recovery would be slow, but it had to begin.

Kiyoko Becomes Kay

Kiyoko was a cute teenager with a pleasant smile. The occupying troops maintained a strong base on the island but were also interested in helping the citizens recover. American soldiers, including military police, helped to restore order. One caught Kiyoko's eye. His name was DeVere. Kiyoko was a normal girl. She realized that all her Okinawan suitors were few and far between, and DeVere was interested in her. They struck up a friendship, and soon, it became more than that. Her mother was for the relationship, but it took longer to convince her father—after all, he had been the enemy. But love prevailed, and the two got married.

Kiyoko became Kay, discovered she would become a mother, and was overjoyed when sweet, adorable Margie was born. Now, finally, here was something of her very own. Her family had lost family members, houses, and possessions, but Kay had little Margie, and they would always have that strong attachment bond.

Travel to the USA

Kay, DeVere, and baby Margie got on a ship and headed for the US. What would life be like for Kay? At least she would have darling Margie. DeVere was from Plymouth, Indiana, and they went there to live with his family. Kay worked to learn English and, in the meantime, had two more children—boys. They were great, but they did not match the bond she shared with Margie.

DeVere and Kay were a happy couple, and they traveled a lot around the United States.

Margie went to grade school, high school, and college. She eventually married and moved to Florida. She and Gerry had a terrific life and a mutual interest in aviation.

One day, Margie got a call from her mother and dad saying they were moving to Florida. They came down and picked out a house. Mother and daughter would be living in the same town again. Life was again great for the family.

But things do happen. DeVere developed dementia, and Kay took care of him until the end. Margie's Gerry also died suddenly. Kay and Margie were by themselves, and the bond between them was even stronger. Margie will soon be the caregiver of Kay.

From Okinawa to Florida, Kay and Margie's bond is unbreakable. What a credit to this mother and daughter!

SMART TIP: In honoring the stories of war brides like Kay, we preserve the legacy of courage and sacrifice that helped shape history. Their tales remind us of the resilience of the human spirit and the enduring power of love, even in the face of adversity.

GUAM: Exotic Surprise and the Simple Life

Valerie Gladhill with Evelyn

John and I are flying to Guam. He is flying for a conference for his business, and I am flying for fun. Although we live in Dallas, Texas, we are originally from England. Hot weather, especially stormy heat, is like a sandbag on the soul, and we understand that Guam is a cut above Dallas in humidity.

Guam is a surprising, exotic place with rich Micronesian history, stunning shores of blinding white sand, and vivid Chamorro culture. After the attack on Pearl Harbor, Japan invaded Guam, a US territory, on December 10, 1941, and instituted a repressive regime. The Imperial Japanese Army had indoctrinated its soldiers to believe that surrender was dishonorable, and prisoners of war were thought to be unworthy of being treated respectfully; it was better to die than be captured. United States forces recaptured the island in 1944.

Day Excursion

My husband's company arranges a day trip with Jim, a retired naval officer who runs a jeep touring company. So we hop into the jeep and plod through the jungle, avoiding bamboo shoots grabbing at our hair and wild pigs darting across the path.

The first stop is in a clearing. "Look over there," Jim says.

We see a World War II Japanese kamikaze dive bomber almost covered with vegetation. "Here is your real surprise."

It is a hole in the ground. We stand like the Moai statues on Easter Island—stone faces, frozen feet. "This is your estate tour of the home of Japanese Sergeant Shoichi Yokoi; he lived in this house for twenty-eight years," Jim says.

He explains that this soldier was dedicated to not surrendering or being captured. First, to hide himself, he had to find a good place. The jungles of the Talofofo River provide great cover, and the soil in the rainforest is shallow and diggable. He dug a hole large enough for him to make a cave in the limestone and made a stand of large, thick, upright bamboo poles, covering it with thatch ground cover. He did not know the war was over then and assumed the worst would happen to him if he were captured.

So he lived in his homemade hole. He became a master at survival. Hunting and fishing at night, he used native plants to make bedding, storage, and clothing. Before he was drafted into the Japanese Army, he was a tailor. He found that palm fronds could make nice clothes with buttons created from coconut shells. His diet was nuts, mangos, papaya, shrimp, snails, frogs, and rats. Water from the Talofofo River quenched his thirst, and he could bathe in the nearby falls.

Back to Japan

One day, two Chamorros, natives of Guam, were checking their shrimp traps along the river and ran into him. The villagers thought he was a native, but he determined his life was in danger and attacked them. They subdued him. He thought they would kill him, but instead, they took him to their houses and gave him warm soup.

He returned to Japan in March 1972 and apologized to his Emperor for losing the war. He knew the war had been over since 1952, but our guide explains how saving face is important in Japanese culture.

In 1982, Yokoi returned to Guam to celebrate the tenth anniversary of his return to living. He appreciated the people of Guam for their respectful treatment and laid a wreath on the grave of Governor Camacho, the person in charge of helping him get back to Japan. In the meantime, he married and became a television guru who promoted simple living. He died of a heart attack in 1997 at the age of eighty-two.

On Guam, a World War II museum tells the story of Sergeant Shoichi Yokoi.

SMART TIP: When traveling for conferences, don't just stay at the hotel. Explore the local culture, history, and natural wonders your host city offers. You never know what fascinating surprises await just beyond the conference rooms.

ISRAEL:
No Worries; It's Okay

By Natalie

This Holy Land for Jews, Christians, and Muslims is one of love, faith, hope, hate, war, and human and divine emotion. I experience all of these emotions on this trip.

The Man Who Changed My View Of Life

My mother and I travel to study the Holy Land with my brother, Kurt, and his theological seminary group. On the flight from New York City to Amman, Jordan, I am seated by a gentleman whom I will call Dr. B. He must have clout, because so many people are trying to introduce themselves to him. In my typical type-A personality fashion, I ask the stranger next to me, "Why are so many people kissing up to you?"

He laughs and says he is a professor at a seminary and taking a class to Israel. "These are my students who want As," he jokes.

I tell him that my brother, Kurt, is in his class, and like a typical sister, I tell the professor to give him an 'F.' We laugh at my brother's expense and talk the entire red-eye flight to Amman. Little do I know that Dr. B will change my views on life.

Unusual Circling

It is still dark as we descend into Amman. We circle the airport several times. I mention my concern about the multiple circling of the airport to Dr. B. He says, "No worries; it's okay."

I continue to watch the flight attendants nervously sweat, and we keep hearing popping sounds. The airplane circles again and does not land.

Pop-pop once again.

And then, a loud BOOM. The flight attendants let out a sigh of relief, and we are cleared to land. As we taxi to the airport on the runway, we ride by police cars and fire trucks. I ask Dr. B, "Do you think that is for us?"

He says, "No worries; it's okay."

The emergency personnel wheel over the mobile stairs to help us disembark the plane. As we wait in line at Customs, we learn that the airport circling was because the plane's wheels would not drop for landing. The pilots and airport control prepared for an emergency landing without the landing gear. The head pilot was ready to announce our emergency landing protocols when the wheels dropped. A "boom" sound will never be the same for me.

Across the Bridge to Israel

We drive over the border into Israel, a tiny land as nations go; only 124 miles long from top to bottom but it drops to 1,312 feet below sea level. It is very arid and rocky. On our way to Qumran, where the Dead Sea Scrolls were discovered, we drive by majestic cliffs of rocks. There are so many sites that I had studied: the desert wilderness; the Sea of Galilee; the Mount of the Beatitudes; Nazareth, where Jesus grew up; and the site of Jesus's baptism in the Jordan River.

One of my most memorable visits is to Bethlehem and the Chapel of the Nativity. It is a once-in-a-lifetime opportunity to go to the very place that historians identify as the birthplace of Jesus. We later see on the news that there had been a demonstration in Bethlehem outside the chapel the same time we were inside—and we never knew it. No worries; it's okay.

We are on our way to Jerusalem and end up at the Dome of the Rock, a gold-domed mosque with a colorful facade in the center of Jerusalem. It is in an area of Muslim control, and one must pass through a checkpoint to enter the mosque. Kurt and mother enter first. I stay behind with Dr. B. The guards block me and will not allow me to enter. From our many travels in Muslim countries, we respect their entry into holy shrines and know proper clothes and shoes. The guard keeps saying No! NO!

Seeing that we will not win the argument, Dr. B says, "No worries; it's okay," and whisks me to the nearest store.

To my surprise, Dr. B. buys me a black choir robe. "Here, put this on over your clothes at the entrance."

Little did I know that the black choir robe is a Burka. With disdain, I cover myself and enter the mosque. I never knew why they wouldn't let me in, but I'm fortunate that Dr. B came to the rescue.

During our last day in Jerusalem, we visit the historic site where scholars believe Jesus was buried. After looking at the spot where Jesus's body rested for three days, we join our group for a sermon by Dr. B. During the last prayer,

The Dome of the Rock: A Jerusalem Gem. Denied entry, Natalie was left to reflect on the tension that ultimately gave way to resolution.

a loud explosion occurs. Boom! Dr. B. says, "No worries; it's okay. It is the start of Ramadan."

We are delayed for several hours on the flight home, so we miss our flight to New York. I would typically have been stressed out, but Dr. B taught me, "No worries; it's okay."

SMART TIP: Always be vigilant and cognizant of your environment. However, do not get stressed about situations out of your control. Trust in your ability to adapt and find solutions, and remember, "No worries; it's okay."

PART 4

Love for Nature, Environment, and the Animal World

The beauty of the world.
Love and courage of animals.
Environment.

ECUADOR:
Movie Stars of the Galapagos

Gravel crunches under our feet as we trek through scrubby trees and sniff the salt breeze from the Pacific Ocean. We have flown to the Galapagos archipelago. We settle on one of the nineteen islands for three days of study and relaxation.

To think, we are in the melting pot of unusual living animals, such as the marine iguanas, the Blue-Footed Booby, and many types of finches—the ones that inspired Charles Darwin to develop his ideas of natural selection following his visit in 1835.

While many of our comrades are enthralled by snorkeling, kayaking, and scuba diving, we have one thought in mind: to see the movie star of the islands—Lonesome George, the Giant Tortoise, and the last of his species.

His ancient brothers were plundered in the 1800s by whalers, fur sealers, and pirates. Tortoise meat was great for sailors because the large, slow animal would stay alive on a ship for up to a year without food or water.

Lonesome George

We walk along with great anticipation, and there he is, the famous tortoise branded as Lonesome George.

George moves as slowly as a snail and seems to have lost some of his luster. His grooming is terrible. His shell looks like a VW bug with dents and algae.

Shining his shell or using some wrinkle cream might make him more attractive to the ladies. Females were placed in his pen in hopes of saving the species. Unfortunately, the females were not interested. They were in the far corner admiring another male tortoise.

Diego, the Stud

In a pen across from Lonesome George is another tortoise, Diego. With his long, thick neck, bright yellow face, and dark eyes, he is among many desperate females. His shell is shiny and aerodynamic like a Porsche; he has lots of charisma. The females love him; Diego has no trouble mating. The biologists explain that Diego has fathered most of the tortoises on that island. Natalie proclaims that she will name her next male dog after Diego. She keeps her promise.

Diego, George's understudy, is now the star. He has single-handedly saved the breeding program and helped increase the tortoise population from fifteen to 2,000.

Update: Lonesome George died on June 24, 2012. He was found dead of natural causes, which surprised his caretakers. He was relatively young for tortoises, which can live over 200 years. Perhaps it was from a lonely, broken heart. His body was sent to the Museum of Natural History in New York for taxidermy, and in 2014, he was returned to the Galapagos and is shown at their nature center.

Meet Diego, the dashing hero of the Galapagos. While the ladies couldn't resist him, Diego's charm went beyond romance—he's credited with saving his species.

SMART TIP: It is desirable to add an excursion to the Galapagos to your trip to Ecuador, Peru, or Chile, or sail with a cruise line around the island. Be sure to see Lonesome George at the museum and say "hello" to Diego from Natalie.

USA, ALASKA,: Calling the Wild

Alaska is the Earth's best scenery, with eons of wind and rain-molded mountains. Looking out of our plane, we are overwhelmed by vast expanses that appear to go on forever. We are on a combination land and sea trip, with the land coming first. We start in Anchorage for an eight-hour train ride to Denali National Park, Alaska's top attraction.

We board the Wilderness Express, a glass-domed train that will be our home for several hours. This train is a flagship because passengers get off and on at any point with the wave of a flag. This is called a hurricane flag stop, where people living in the bush can get transportation, since no major roads exist.

Although the scenery is spectacular, one of our main goals in travel is to learn about the culture, people, and history that make the place. We look for things not in the travel books—although they are the beginning of inspiration.

Mayor Stubbs

One of the stops is at Talkeetna, a village of 900 residents. In 1997, no one wanted to run for mayor, so the people elected Stubbs the cat. The cat was mayor until 2017, when he died from an injury from a dog attack. Throughout December, this town also sponsors a Wilderness Woman competition. Women haul five-gallon buckets up and down the main street, chop wood, and drive snowmobiles. This qualifies them for the bachelor auction to raise money for their charities.

Denali National Park

We arrive at Denali National Park. In the background is marvelous Mount Denali. We know it from its pictures, but unfortunately, we cannot see it through the rain and dense fog. Mount Denali, also known as the tall one, was called Mount McKinley for many years in honor of President William McKinley. Denali was the original name of the Athabaskan language, and in 2005, it was officially changed back to this name.

Denali is the tallest mountain in North America, peaking at 20,210 feet. About 1,000 adventurers attempt to climb it yearly—about half make it. The trip takes between seventeen to twenty-one days. We decide to skip this adventure.

We are loaded on an old school bus that takes admirers around the park. We enjoy seeing the wildlife and spotting the big five: moose, caribou, black bear, Dall sheep, and wolf. We see an abundance of ptarmigans, Alaska's state birds. They are brown now, but in the winter they will turn white to blend in with the snow background.

To Fairbanks

Now we are in our comfortable coach, heading toward Fairbanks. One of the exciting road experiences is a stop at the Tatanika Campground. Standing by the giant black wood stove, we talk with the owner, Jay, a native who lives in the campground year-round, about Alaska politics. He was six when Alaska became a state; it was a thrilling time with lots of celebration and wonder for a small boy. He was pleased to hear us ask about Alaska politics because we are the first tourists to do so. They have issues similar to many places: large cities and interests take precedence over less populated areas.

We go across the Teklanika River, made famous by the saga of Chris McCandless, the twenty-four-year-old who emulated Henry David Thoreau and Jack London to leave civilization and live in the wild. He was less fortunate. When he first went across the river, it was low and could be walked easily across. However, when snow begins to melt, it becomes a raging torrent and impossible to cross. He found an old school bus and discovered that living off the land was not good and decided to go back across the river, but it was too swollen to cross. Officially, he died of starvation, but there is some debate as to the exact cause of his death. We pass by the University of Alaska, Fairbanks, where the bus is now displayed in a museum.

Black Gold

We are used to hearing news reports about the Trans-Alaska pipeline. We stand under it at a point where it passes above ground. The pipeline encounters various environmental challenges on its 800-mile journey from Prudhoe Bay in the far north to Valdez. Sometimes it is underground, and at other times it is above ground.

Panning for Gold

Now is our time to be real Stampeders and pan for gold. For us visitors, they make the experience as authentic as possible. We are not in the creek moiling for gold, but in a shed. We are given a little baggie of dirt and led to the heated water trough. We empty our dirt into a pan and start washing. You are instructed to hold the pan at an angle and slosh up and down, letting the water wash out the dirt. Gold nugget bits are left. We take them to be weighed. Evelyn has $6; Natalie, $30.

Skagway

After five days, we join the cruise ship for the rest of our Alaskan adventure. Great scenery, including the famous Glacier Bay, Ketchikan, and the largest collection of totem poles await us.

SMART TIP: Although being on the big ship is generally relaxing with lots of food and drink, we encourage people who want to see and know Alaska to plan to travel overland to Denali, Fairbanks, and the Yukon. You will experience the true call of the wild.

ALASKA, U.S: Man's Best Friend

"Here, Kusko, here, boy."

Kusko wags his tail as he greets us at the edge of his spacious pen. We talk to the docile leader of the pack. Like the other ranger dogs, he has a house and plenty of room for exercise. In the pen, he is calm and friendly. However, as we take our seats and view from the bleachers, the rangers lead the dogs out of the pen. What a personality change! They begin jumping like Jack-in-the-boxes, pulling the leaders, and tap dancing on the pavement. When they are harnessed up, they are rarin' to go. The ranger tells them when to mush, and then they are off to the races, pulling the snow sled along.

Kusko is one of the canine rangers that connect the past to the present. The sled dogs perform essential wintertime duties in the vast two million acres of designated wilderness in Denali. They are a great alternative to motorized transport for going into the areas since

Alaska's Sled Dogs: The Unsung Heroes of Denali. With no powered vehicles allowed in the park, these hardworking canines are trained to tackle everything—from hauling supplies to search and rescue. Kusko is waiting to lead the sled team.

snowmobiles are banned in the park. The dogs assist with scientific research, transporting supplies, checking up on bush residents, and maintaining a ranger presence for winter visitors. They not only protect the wilderness but help carry on history and tradition.

Thirty-four dogs are kept. New puppies raised by special kennels learn to run with the big dogs yearly. Older dogs retire and are in demand for adoption.

Balto

1925: the people of Nome were desperate. A deadly outbreak of diphtheria had reared its ugly head, and the only medicine available was in Anchorage, 1,000 miles away. The fur-wrapped serum was first sent by rail to Nenana; then, dogs came to the rescue. They had to travel 674 miles to Nome across some of the roughest and coldest terrain on Earth. The snow was blowing; a terrible blizzard made it impossible for the human driver to see. But Balto persevered and arrived at 5:30 a.m. on February 2. Balto received a hero's welcome, and the town was saved.

We see a statue of Balto as we depart from Fairbanks. There is also a bronze statue in New York City's Central Park. The inscription reads:

ENDURANCE—FIDELITY—INTELLIGENCE

The Iditarod and Yukon Quest

In March, mushers and a team of twelve to fourteen dogs participate in the annual long-distance sled dog race from Anchorage to Nome. They must cover the distance in eight to fifteen days or more, and at least five dogs must be on the towline at the finish line. These are terrible days for travel. Teams often must go through blizzards with white-out conditions, face sub-zero temperatures, and endure wind chill that may cause the temperature to be minus 100 degrees

Fahrenheit. A great ceremony and prizes for the human musher are held at the end.

Some animal protection activists say this is not a commemoration of the 1925 serum delivery, but instead declare that it is cruelty to animals. Several dogs have died or been injured during the race. Recently, some people have decided not to participate, and some companies have withdrawn their sponsorship.

The Yukon Quest is another race from Fairbanks, Alaska, to Whitehorse, Yukon. This 1,000-mile race has been dubbed "the toughest race in the world." It follows the course of the historic Klondike Gold Rush. Ten checkpoints are 200 miles apart and lie along the trail. Veterinarians are present and may remove a dog or team for medical or other reasons.

The use of dogs for work as rangers is certainly admirable and well-supervised. We heard that people living in other parts of Alaska or the Yukon use dogs because their snowmobiles are unpredictable in very low temperatures.

SMART TIP: Don't miss visiting a kennel where sled dogs are trained.

SCOTLAND, USA., SOUTH AFRICA: Dedicated Dogs

While traveling, we cannot take our dogs with us, but we are still enamored when we see statues of dogs, which immediately evoke "oohs" and "aahs." Some dogs have important stories; others were important enough to some people to deserve a bronze statue.

There are other statues in many countries that we have not seen. However, we want to honor some dedicated dogs we have experienced in our travels.

Greyfriars Bobby

Have you met the most famous statue of a dog in the world? We'll take you to Edinburgh, Scotland. Bobby, an adorable black Skye Terrier, sits on a round pedestal made of a stone mosaic and capped with a crown.

John Gray, a simple night watchman, had a faithful dog named Bobby who followed him everywhere. John died and was buried in the Greyfriars Churchyard. For the next fourteen years, the little terrier stood guard over his master's grave until he died. The story charmed an English noblewoman who erected a drinking fountain with a statue on top. You can find the dog's statue along Candlemaker Row near the cemetery known as Greyfriars Kirk. Books and movies have honored Bobby.

Fala

There are three statues of Fala in different parts of the United States. We have seen Fala in the Roosevelt Memorial in Washington, D.C. Franklin Roosevelt, our thirty-second president, looks noble and confident in his chair. Beside him is Fala, who also looks noble and confident. President Roosevelt took his little black Scottish terrier everywhere, sometimes receiving criticism for doing so.

Just Nuisance

We are in Simon's Town, South Africa, and run upon this marvelous statue of a Great Dane overlooking the town waterfront. He was called Nuisance because he was always there and followed the sailors everywhere. The sailors fed him snacks and took him for a walk. He was enlisted officially in the Royal Navy during World War II. Because he was so large, he got his name from lying across the gangplank, presenting a "nuisance" for anyone wanting to get around.

Nuisance became Just Nuisance. He was promoted from Ordinary Seaman to Able Seaman and given a sailor's cap from the HMS Canberra. Later, he was hit by an automobile and paralyzed, necessitating his discharge from the Navy. When he died, he was buried with full military honors and memorialized with a regal statue.

Molly, Animal Ambassador

Molly, a white mixed breed canine, became the ambassador for the Marion County, Florida, animal abuser data base known as Molly's Law. Molly had lived a rough life. She was stabbed three times in the head and had her skull fractured in early 2014. Her attacker has served time in state prison on three counts of cruelty to animals. This act of inhumanity led citizens to say that something must be done.

This registry, known as Molly's Law, requires convicted offender to be placed on a registry that allows citizens, pet sellers, and rescue organizations to verify they are not placing a dog with an animal abuser.

Molly lived to be fifteen and was a happy canine until the end with her new owners. Citizens have created a statue of Molly that proudly stands in downtown Ocala, Florida.

We are including this article on dedicated dogs for the owners and pets whose bond is like no other. Dogs are our friends regardless of what the world throws at us. Dogs show us joy, make us laugh, and listen to us like they know exactly what we are saying. Some dogs are memorialized in stone; others are just remembered in love.

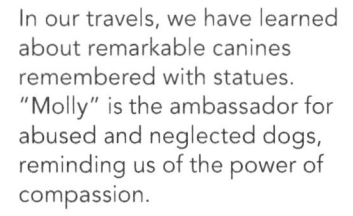

In our travels, we have learned about remarkable canines remembered with statues. "Molly" is the ambassador for abused and neglected dogs, reminding us of the power of compassion.

SMART TIP: Before making specific travel plans, check with your pet lodge or pet sitter about lodging availability.

ROMANIA:
The Dogs of Bucharest

In 1995, we made Bucharest, the capital of Romania, the final stop in our Eastern European tour. This city was once considered the Paris of the East, with its Triumphal Arch (Arcul de Triump) and exciting past.

Our hotel is the historic Athenee Palace, a center of espionage during World Wars I and II. Spies had small orifices in the ceiling and floors that enabled them to hear what was transpiring on the other floors. In the lobby, a person who whispers at one end of the room can be heard at the other.

We discover the superb acoustics that night. We have just jumped into bed when we hear mournful howling, like "the call of the wild." There is yipping, yelping, crying, and growling. We are experiencing a true dogfight—and it sounds like we are in the midst of it. Growls and cries continue all night long.

The following day, our guide tells us to watch for the Roma people and not to feed the dogs. He explains that beginning about 1965, the communist leader Nicolae Ceausescu forced people to move from their homes into communist apartment blocks. They had to abandon their dogs, and the legislature passed laws forbidding euthanasia. The street dogs multiplied and formed packs; we had heard a fight between rival dog gangs last night.

Fast forward to 2015, and we schedule a trip to Transylvania. That means staying at the Athenee Palace Hotel in Bucharest for two nights. What? There are no dog fights. What is the difference?

People loved their animals, but the dogs were becoming aggressive and many citizens and tourists were attacked. On September 2, 2013, a pack of dogs mauled and killed a four-year-old boy while he was playing in the park. The attack caused a public outcry, and laws were quickly passed to adopt, sterilize, or humanely care for the dogs.

Now, Bucharest is a thriving, bustling city full of outdoor cafes where families are safe and their dogs are on leashes. There are no longer packs of dogs roaming the streets and fighting at night.

SMART TIP: Explore Bucharest's transformation from the "Paris of the East" to a thriving city. Embrace the charm of this unique city, where responsible pet ownership has contributed to a more harmonious urban environment.

USA: Blue Dog

We are in New Orleans for an overnight stay in the Intercontinental Hotel. On this trip, we encounter the paintings of Blue Dog for the first time in the hotel lobby. Calling Natalie over, I say, "Look at these paintings; these dogs have the most unusual eyes. Blue dog is in the same pose each time."

We are looking at him from the front; he is a ghostly, terrier-like blue dog with a white nose and mesmerizing yellow eyes. However, the background of the dog changes. He may be standing next to a red alligator on a sandy beach with palm trees or in the forest with live oak trees and Spanish moss swishing in the breeze.

So, where did all these blue dogs come from? They are the handiwork of Louisiana artist George Rodrigue. In 1980, George was recruited to contribute to a book on ghost stories at the 1984 World's Fair. He was known for his folksy, Cajun paintings of an evil dog who was part wolf. This creature was known as loup-garou. He had red eyes and blue-grey fur, and George called the painting "Watchdog." The painting was a hit at the fair, but the image of this dog-wolf was about to change.

The Cajun legend of loup-garou was a scary tale and part of the ghost stories he heard growing up in Southwest Louisiana. The tale was transported to Louisiana when French Canadians were forced to leave Nova Scotia and found their way to the bayous. Loup-garou was a popular figure in French Canadian and European folklore. Who is he? Loup-garou is a werewolf-like dog or a lycanthrope; it can also become human. Like many fairy tales, it is passed on from generation to generation in the dark of night to keep children from misbehaving. If they do not do what they should, loup-garou may be there.

One day, while shuffling through some photographs, George came upon a picture of Tiffany, his beloved dog. Tiffany, a small terrier spaniel, looked straight at the camera with her perky ears straight up. She was black with a white streak running from the top of the head across her nose.

George came up with the idea: why not use Tiffany as my model? He would change the dog's eyes from red to yellow, and the grey-blue of the shadows of night became all shades of blue. Now he had his Blue Dog. Painting all sorts of backgrounds and landscapes became the changing angle.

Blue Dog has become an icon of pop culture. If you go to George's studio, you will see him in all backgrounds, from riding motorcycles to patriotic portraits. One comic poster had him speak: "Sometimes I feel like a blue dog."

George died in 2013, but his creative legacy lives on in the pop art he created.

Meet Blue Dog: With ghostly blue fur, a white nose, and mesmerizing yellow eyes, he's an icon of Louisiana's vibrant culture. Painted in whimsical settings—from a beach with a red alligator to beneath a moss-draped oak—Blue Dog is the unforgettable creation of Cajun artist George Rodrigue.

SMART TIP: If you ever get to look up the paintings or go to an exhibit by George Rodrigue with Blue Dog, you will be amazed how this one dog icon can fit into many different backgrounds.

GREECE:
Cats of the Acropolis

We are in Athens at the base of the Acropolis. "Oh, look at the little black and white kitty," Natalie says.

We saw the sign that said not to pet the animals, but this one is so cute and tempting. Then, a tabby cat and a poor one with a deformed foot crosses our path. Another has several extra toes.

We talk to a lady on a park bench. She tells us that she has sought peace by bringing her lunch to eat outside. Then, suddenly there are twenty cats. No peace here.

It is a scorching afternoon in August when the bus drops us off at the foot of the Acropolis. Oh! A cat crosses our path, then another with all kinds and colors. I remember the children's story, *Millions of Cats*, and the refrain: "Cats here, cats there, cats and kittens everywhere."

Our thought is that we cannot take any more of these cats. Please get us away from this hot place and these cats and back to Florida.

My remembrance of the Acropolis focuses on the oppressive heat and the many cats.

Twenty years later, we return to Greece. We start in Athens, and the Acropolis is our first visit. It is also August, but we climb the steep hill in the morning. The cats are still there—seemingly millions of them. But my attitude is different. As we march through the Propylaea gate, I am thrilled to see the Parthenon, the small Temple of Athena Nike, and the museum with its many artifacts. We talk to the cats as they weave freely in and out.

When we join the group, we ask the guide about the cats. He informs us that Greeks love their cats. Efforts to control them have failed because many citizens think it is cruel to neuter them and impede their freedom. Cats roam freely all over Greece, with the largest population on the Greek island of Santorini.

We were fortunate to study the classics twice in Greece and the Acropolis. As for the cats, they will still be there in twenty years, fifty years, or even one hundred years.

SMART TIP: Expect to see cats when visiting Greece, Turkey, or other Mediterranean sites. Just accept them as part of the environment and culture.

USA, GREECE, RUSSIA: For the Love of Horses

"Please don't take my horse. He is my only friend and the only thing I have left," Bobby said. "Take anything else—but don't take my horse."

The Union Soldier looked at him, sneered, and grabbed the horse's bridle out of his hand. After all, General Sherman's march through Georgia depended upon living on the land, and horses were necessary for soldiers.

Bobby again pleaded but to no avail. He watched as the soldier pulled the unwilling horse to join the others. Tears streamed down his face as he followed them down the road until the soldier and the horse disappeared around the bend on the dusty red Georgia road.

My friend Angela told me this story. Bobby was her grandfather, and he told this story over and over. Angela and her husband own a farm in the heart of horse country in Marion County, Florida. Bobby's love for horses has transferred to her.

One cannot imagine the pull of the love of the horse. A horse plays a different role for different people—companion, friend, and sports. We relate the stories of famous equestrian statues we have seen in our travels. We could have included a long list but settled on three.

Alexander the Great and Bucephalus, Thessaloniki, Greece

Alexander's father, Philip II, gave this wild, undisciplined horse to the boy. No one could manage him. However, Alexander took up the challenge to tame him. People laughed that a mere boy would attempt to manage this spirited horse because none of them could do so. Alexander observed that the horse was frightened of his own shadow. He would back away and even lie down when he would see it. So Alex gently turned his head toward the sun and was able to mount him and even put a bridle on him.

He was only twenty years old and had spent most of his life fighting. When his father was assassinated, he became king and military leader of a great army. He conquered the great Persian empire, and it is said that he cried when he had no more lands to conquer.

Part of his world was his dear horse, Bucephalus. He was black with a large white star on his forehead and a large head. He had a true bond with his horse; they were inseparable. He was the only one who could ride him and took him into every battle. Most historians think Bucephala died of old age; some say of battle wounds. In mourning, Alex named a city after him, Bucephala (now the modern city of Jhelum in Pakistan).

We saw this statue of Alexander the Great mounted on Bucephalus in Thessaloniki, Greece. This bronze equestrian statue stands twenty feet high. This is one of the best-known statues in the world.

Peter the Great: The Bronze Horseman

When we travel to Saint Petersburg, Russia, we see the magnificent equestrian statue of Peter the Great. This statue was commissioned by Catherine the Great and opened to the public in 1782. The pedestal is called the Thunder Stone. It is the largest stone ever moved by humans and weighs 1,500 tons. It is not determined whether Peter had any great affection for his horse, but the rearing steed on the rough-hewn stone means so much to the people of this city. When it was under siege for 900 days during World War II, the statue was covered with sandbags and had a shelter to protect it from bombing and fire.

Sergeant Reckless World Equestrian Center, Ocala, Florida

It was October 1952, and a little stable boy in Seoul, Korea, needed money to buy an artificial leg for his sister. He had a charming chestnut-colored mare that had a blaze on her forehead and three white stockings. Some Marines bought the horse for $250 to make her a pack horse for a platoon. Quickly, this horse was given the name Reckless, and she became part of the unit. She could roam around freely and eat anything, including poker chips.

During the Korean conflict, she carried supplies and munitions; she was also known to help evacuate the wounded, even without the guidance of another Marine. In March of 1953, during the Battle for Outpost Vegas, she made fifty-one trips in a single day. Wounded twice, she was given the rank of corporal and later sergeant. Her military honors were legion.

She was awarded two Purple Hearts and other medals that she could wear on her horse blanket for her bravery in service. Monuments to Reckless are many. Her latest one is at the World Equestrian Center in Ocala, Florida.

We are often under fire—not from armies but from the arrows of life. Stories of these statues can give us meaning and encouragement to endure what we may encounter.

A Tribute to a True Friend: This statue of Restless, a heroine of the Korean conflict, stands proudly at the World Equestrian Center in Ocala, Florida. A reminder of the loyalty and bravery horses have shown through the ages.

SMART TIP: Learn from the bravery and courage of animals and their masters. Horses are highly perceptive animals with keen instincts and cognitive abilities. By respecting and tapping into the natural intelligence of a horse, you'll build a stronger bond and achieve greater harmony in your partnership.

BULGARIA:
The Dancing Bears

In the nineteenth and early twentieth centuries, bears were used for entertainment in many US and European towns. An announcement would go out through the community, inviting anyone who wanted to wrestle the bear to take a turn trying to do so. Paul Bryant was thirteen years old, six feet one inch tall, and very tough. At the Lyric Theater in Fordyce, Arkansas, an ad read that anyone who wrestled a bear for one minute could win a dollar. Paul volunteered and wrestled for a complete minute, but the owner and the bear escaped without paying. This adventure earned him the nickname Paul "Bear" Bryant, a famous University of Alabama football coach.

We are traveling over roads with deep ruts and cavernous pits from Sophia, the capital of Bulgaria, to an overnight stay in a small village on the Turkish border. As we arrive at our destination, we see a crowd gathered. A man wearing an embroidered red vest over a tan shirt and a black hat shaped like an ice cream cone with the tip cut off is calling people to come. He has a huge brown bear with a ring in its nose on a short chain. Holding his bow at the waist, he plays upbeat music on a small stringed instrument called a gadulka. The bear starts to dance, and the crowd goes wild. They throw coins and bills, which his family picks up.

Someone speaks to us in English and asks. "What do you think of the dancing bears?"

He identifies himself as an animal rights group member trying to ban this practice.

How Bears Learn to Dance

He tells us this story:

Dancing bears have been seen in Europe for ages. The royalty brought their children to see the bears in Bulgaria. The craft of training bears is passed on from generation to generation of Roma buskers. They capture a baby bear and tie it down for days without water and food. Then, the master gives it food and water. They declaw the animal and put a ring through the most sensitive body part, his nose. The bear is forced to step on hot plates. He lifts his sensitive feet one step at a time to avoid getting burned while the owner plays music. The bear develops the conditioned reflex link between the hot plates and music. He begins to lift his paws, which looks like a dance. So now, when the music starts, he jumps and dances. The bears are fed bread and sweets mixed with vodka or beer, and many die of malnourishment. Bread and vodka are not their native diet.

We are horrified—especially when we hear how they train these bears.

Bulgaria banned bear dancing in 1998, responding to pressure from animal rights groups. The Four Paws Brigette Bardot Foundation bought land in the Bulgarian mountains and called it "Belitsa Sanctuary." The last Bulgarian dancing bear was rescued in 2007. In 2017, a bear from Albania was rescued—he was likely Europe's last dancing bear.

SMART TIP: Many other animals are still being abused in the world. For example, cock and dog fighting. Support reputable animal rights groups that are helping abused and neglected animals.

BRAZIL:
The Amazon Experience

We arrive in Manaus late at night and go to the Go Inn. As the sun peeps above the horizon, we see this city of 2 million, the capital of the state of Amazonia.

Manaus

"Wow, I am overwhelmed," exclaims Natalie. "Here we are, thousands of miles from home in a city known as the 'Paris of the Amazon.' What a place amid the jungle."

We stroll along the plaza which has a striking pavement pattern. If you've seen pictures or been to the Copacabana in Rio de Janeiro, you have seen the famous wavy mosaic pavement in black and white marble. A similar pattern is the Calcadao da Ponta Negra, a beautiful mosaic made of Portuguese cobblestones. The cobblestones are arranged to create intricate patterns, which are said to be from old Portuguese folk art.

Still in the plaza, we stand with mouths agape, looking at the majestic Teatro Amazonas, that nineteenth-century opera house that brought the grandeur of Europe to the heart of Brazil. The building is pink with white pillars holding it up. What is that on top? A dome. This top is emblazoned with the blue, green, and gold Brazilian flag, created with 36,000 imported tiles. Some citizens do not like the dome, and we think that it does look a little out of place.

Although it is Christmas Day, our guide takes us to see the interior. We sit in the curved auditorium shaped like a lyre. There are 198 Italian chandeliers and Venetian Murano glass. The terrific acoustics result from Scottish cast iron that holds up twenty-two hollow columns. In its first two decades, the house attracted artists from around Europe.

We wander around the streets, hoping to meet a rubber baron. A little history: the invention of the automobile in the late nineteenth century started the demand for rubber. The boom began. Manaus, a small dumpy river town, blossomed into a metropolitan city of class and refinement.

The rich and famous demanded Brazil's first telephone system, sixteen miles of streetcar tracks, and an electric grid. Flaunting wealth became a sport. The rubber barons are said to have lit cigars with $100 bills and watered their horses with silver buckets of chilled French champagne. Their wives would not wash clothes in the muddy waters of the Amazon; they sent them to Europe to be laundered. Imported food provided opulent dinners, after which the gentlemen would retire to an elegant bordello.

Meeting of the Waters

We wake up early to see the fascinating Meeting of the Waters phenomenon. Rio Negro River is black with slow-running water from the Colombian hills and Andes Mountains, and contains decayed leaves and plant matter. The Solimoes River is pale, sandy white, faster moving, and lower in temperature. The rivers flow side-by-side without combining for about six miles before mixing to become the Amazon.

Back in Manaus, we are ready for a treat. Almost all restaurants show pictures of their famous dessert: Meeting of Waters. The yummy treat has brown pudding on one side and vanilla on the other. When you prepare to eat it, you mix the two puddings to simulate the mixing of the waters.

A Mesmerizing Sight in Brazil: The dark waters of the Rio Negro and the white waters of the Solimões River flow side by side for miles without mixing—just one of the many wonders Brazil has in store for the adventurous traveler.

SMART TIP: The Blue Ribbon Award for Best World Dessert goes to the MEETING OF WATERS in Manaus, Brazil. It is a must have.

NICARAGUA: Land of Volcanoes, Lakes, and Castrated Raccoons

A lilting song of the 1940s proclaimed what a wonderful spot Managua, Nicaragua, was. That was what people knew about Nicaragua in the 1940s. However, if we asked you what you know about Nicaragua today, you would probably say Sandinista/Contra battles and people fleeing the country.

This characterization is such a shame. It does have a bloody and gory history, but it is a relatively safe place when we visit this country in 2014. The people had willingly given up their guns in exchange for beans and rice. These guns are embedded in a concrete wall in Charmarro's Peace Park in Managua. However, political changes appear to be the norm in this country.

Berman, the TV Star

Our guide is Berman, a native, and he stays with us throughout our visit to Nicaragua. Berman is a "television star," a consultant, and a guide for the reality TV show. He knows the jungles like the back of his hand.

We are in Granada, our favorite beauty spot, surrounded by three volcanoes; we see fire, but there have been no eruptions since 1976. Colonial cities are built around a square, surrounded by the cathedral, government buildings, shops, and homes of the wealthy. These homes have been converted to boutique hotels; we stay in one of those.

We walk into the plaza. There are fireworks, music, dancing, streamers, and a grand celebration with food and people selling souvenirs. The government is negotiating with China to build a canal for shipping across Lake Nicaragua. The canal was to begin construction on December 22, 2014, and be completed by 2020. The government is happy; the people and environmentalists are not. The project could destroy a great ecosystem. In 2024, although the idea is still being floated, the canal has been stopped.

Nicaragua is one of the world's most diverse areas of plants and animals. There are 7,000 different plants and 750 different kinds of birds. People come from all over the world to study the local flora and fauna.

Berman takes us for a boat ride on Lake Nicaragua, showing us the canal's path. This lake has 350 small volcanic islands.

"Stop!" Berman says. "Do you see that long green line over there on that rock wall?" We look. Berman jumps out of the boat and climbs onto the rocks. He picks up a green vine snake that is at least three feet longer than Berman is tall. This is all in a day's work for him.

Grenada to Leon

It's time to move on to Grenada's rival, Leon. It does not have the charm of Granada, but it is still interesting. We stay in another boutique hotel, El Convento, a former nunnery. Like all convents, there is a large courtyard and places for meditation; our room is where nuns stayed.

On the way to Leon, we pass through Diriomo, the town of real witches. They are famous for their love potion. The witch procures a raccoon penis, dries it, pulverizes it to a powder, and puts in a drink. It never fails, you will fall in love. Don't put too much powder in the drink or the person will go crazy.

SMART TIP: Although there are many ways to travel to a country, we highly recommend traveling with an organized and reputable travel company, especially if you are traveling to more vulnerable countries.

FRANCE: Claude Monet—From Class Clown to Nature Lover

In school, Claude Monet was the class clown who had a great sense of humor. Class clowns are a special type with the same characteristics. They are not mean, but they do enjoy making people laugh. They look around to see whose eyes they can catch to make them laugh. They usually do not do too well in school, which would keep them from clowning. Fitting this class clown mold, Monet did not do well in school because he spent his time drawing funny pictures. His teachers—especially their noses—were his targets.

Out in Nature

Later, some people in town thought he was so good at drawing caricatures that they paid him for their pictures. He loved drawing, but an artist, Eugene Boudin, had some strange ideas about painting. Instead of being stuck in a stuffy studio, he believed that artists should paint outside. That suited Monet well; he loved nature. And with the invention of oil paint in tubes, he could carry them outside.

From the river cruise, we take a bus to Giverny. We see the house where he lived, walk where Monet walked, and go into his gardens. We are pleased to be in nature with him.

We also fight the establishment with him. The powerful wanted paintings that told stories of battles, mythology, or historical events—and they wanted them painted in dark colors.

But Monet liked painting with light colors and simple subjects like boats on a lake, oceans, or even a haystack in the field. Once, he painted the sunrise with a boat on a shimmering lake. He called the painting "Impression: Sunrise." Little did he know that he would name the movement he loved. He even built a special boat to travel up and down rivers and streams to paint outside.

Monet's House and Gardens

When walking through the house at Giverny, we are impressed by its simplicity, especially for dining. It is simple and homey, unlike some of the other places we had visited, such as the luxurious Versailles. The house is painted pink with green shutters. He had a trellis for climbing roses, and Virginia creepers grew on the house. He wanted the house to blend with nature.

The most majestic part of Giverny is Monet's gardens. We walk from path to path through the magnificent grounds so eloquently kept. We follow the most popular path to the water garden and the Japanese bridge. He spent the last ten years of his life painting scenes of his water garden.

What we appreciate most is his love of nature and the fact that you can enjoy it even through mist and fog. He wanted to show how things looked momentarily—just as a camera does. We experience this snapshot in time at the Japanese bridge.

Claude Monet taught the world to see and love nature and is considered the "Father of Impressionism." His paintings have no story to tell nor any moral instruction, and these impressions and sensations were painted outside rather than in a stuffy studio.

From class clown to the Father of Impressionism, Monet was a maverick of his time.

SMART TIP: Accept your inner maverick and find inspiration in nature's beauty, just as Monet did. Don't be afraid to challenge conventions. Like Monet, let the world around you ignite your passion.

TUNISIA:
Humps, Lumps, and BMWs

A highlight of any trip to the Middle East—Morocco, Tunisia, Jordan, or Egypt—is riding a camel. At the very least, you must take a picture of your mount to show everyone back home.

Sahara Desert Camels

We are in Tunisia, riding through the Sahara desert. We pass old tanks and the vestigial remains of World War II desert battles, but that is not what we are excited about. We will soon reach the camel farm for a thirty-minute ride into the desert and back.

Approaching the farm, we hear mournful bellowing and loud grunts that remind us of the *Call of the Wild*. Females are in season, and the males are calling. However, they are separated; we will be riding male camels.

For centuries, camels, known as the ships of the desert, have had great social, sports, recreation, milk, meat, fiber, and transportation significance. In Morocco, one guy told me he would trade three camels for my daughter Natalie. She laughed and asked, "Am I only worth three?"

He assured her that "camels are like BMWs" and are worth lots of money.

Dressing Like a Bedouin

We don special long gowns the color of light brown sugar and wrap our heads with bathroom towels—like the ones shepherds wear in Christmas pageants. We are no longer tourists but true Bedouins riding the magnificent ships of the desert.

One of the grooms confides to Natalie that he will get her the BMW of camels: the best riding one. She mounts the BMW's single hump, which is covered with a packed bundle of rags that look like recent acquisitions from the thrift store. He is on his knees and looks happy as she climbs aboard, as if he wants her to be as comfortable as possible.

Not so with my camel. He screams and spits and immediately does not like me, and I don't care for him, either. He has a bad attitude. I have heard camels can be hostile to humans. I attempt to mount, but the lumpy bundle pack keeps slipping. I ask for another camel with a better personality. My new camel is mild-mannered and laid back. I ride with joy and even have my picture taken with him.

However, half an hour can be a lifetime on your hips and joints when sitting in a rocking chariot hanging onto the saddle's horn. At least I made it for thirty minutes.

A Camel Ride Is a Must for Any Adventurer: Dressed as Bedouins, we fully embraced the desert spirit and captured the unforgettable experience.

Jan, another party member, is stuck with my camel reject. He does not like her, either. He behaves like a disgruntled child, slinging his head and stumbling, trying to throw her off balance. He keeps swishing his tail upon her back. She walks a miserable thirty minutes with him. When she dismounts, all up and down the back of her outfit are dark brown streaks—of unmentioned origin. That camel was not a BMW, it was more like a Ford Pinto, with back-end explosions and all.

We learn that camels, like people, have feelings, moods, and unpredictable personalities. They have reputations of being bad-tempered and obstinate because they fear being abused. Some specialists say this assessment is not fair. They are smart and have the intellect and emotional intelligence of an eight-year-old child. Living in herds led by a dominant male, they greet each other by blowing in one another's faces.

SMART TIP: If you are going to ride a camel, be smart and ask for the BMW.

PART 5

Love for Education and Lifelong Learning

History, Art, Science, Geography, Sites.

EGYPT: Mummy and Daughter in Search of Imhotep

By Natalie

My favorite movie of all time is the 1999 version of *The Mummy*. The High Priest Imhotep fascinated me in this movie, so I had to go to Egypt to learn more about him. That happened in 2005 when we traveled to the land of the great Pharaohs.

Pyramids of Giza

Our trek starts at the Great Pyramids. Our guide's name is Mohammed, AKA Medo. He is an exceptional Egyptologist who studied under masters. He takes us to the Sphinx, a forty-foot statue of Pharaoh Khafre guarding the pyramids. The overwhelming grandeur of the Great Pyramids is breathtaking. One can only imagine how these gigantic structures were designed to prepare the pharaoh for the afterlife and were constructed without modern technology, which brings us closer to Imhotep.

Sakkara: The First Pyramid

Medo takes us south of Giza to the simplistic pyramid of Sakkara—the first known pyramid. Built two hundred years before the pyramids of Giza, Sakkara, also known as the Step Pyramid, is small and unimpressive. It was designed to prepare King Djoser for the afterlife and included mummified pets, animals, and the pharaoh's food.

Here, I follow in the footsteps of Imhotep. As a chancellor to King Djoser, Imhotep created an architectural miracle, Sakkara. He developed granite burial chambers, false doors, and mazes of false corridors to protect the pharaohs for the afterlife. Imhotep is the reason we have so much information about ancient Egypt. Therefore, we have an understanding of how these pharaohs lived.

Who was Imhotep (2655-2600 BCE)? He was a polymath who was knowledgeable in many fields. In addition to being the chancellor to Pharaoh Djoser, he was the high priest of the Sun God Ra at Heliopolis. Considered the first architect, engineer, and physician in recorded history, he was one of the few commoners ever considered divine by the Egyptian people. Even the Greeks deified him as Asclepius, the god of healing.

No More Magic

It is said that Imhotep should be the "father of medicine." Instead of taking the Hippocratic Oath, doctors could be taking the "Imhotepic Oath." Unlike others in his era, Imhotep was devoid of magical thinking. He challenged the ideas that illnesses were caused by some higher power or maybe an adversary. He treated such things as broken bones or crocodile bites with specific treatments. Infections could be cured with honey.

What Is a Mummy?

While we are at the step pyramid, Medo conducts a session on how mummies were made. Mummification began around 2,600 BC. It occurs when a person or animal has soft tissue preserved.

The process probably followed this procedure:

- Removing the brain
- Storing the internal organs—liver, lungs, stomach, and intestines—in separate canopic jars
- Removing the most important organ—the heart
- Covering the body inside and out with natron salts
- Wrapping the body with linen
- Adorning the body with amulets
- Placing the wrapped body in a sarcophagus shaped like a human body

According to Egyptian mythology, the heart is weighed against the feather of the goddess Maat to measure whether the person's soul will reach the afterlife.

Power of Imhotep Today

Many organizations, including universities, have used his name for various purposes. These groups involve wisdom and intellect with this historical figure.

The more I know and study about Imhotep, the more I appreciate him. I especially thank him for being the protagonist of my favorite movie, *The Mummy*.

SMART TIP: Learn more about this Egyptian polymath. Some universities, schools, or educational programs name clubs, societies, or lecture series after Imhotep, particularly those focusing on architecture, engineering, medicine, or Egyptology.

MEXICO:
The Day of the Dead

We are in Oaxaca, Mexico, and chatting with a group at the dinner table.

"Tell us about Cinco de Mayo, your Independence Day."

Their faces look like we are going up the down staircase.

"No, no, no, that is not our Independence Day. Our Independence Day is September 16. In 1821, Father Hidalgo led the nation into freeing us from that oppressor Spain."

We are informed that Cinco de Mayo is more prevalent in the US than in Mexico and is celebrated in only one city, Puebla, where 2,000 Mexican soldiers defeated 6,000 invading French troops.

We show our lack of knowledge when they mention a holiday they had just celebrated on November 1 and 2: Dia de los Muertos, the Day of the Dead.

We have Halloween, but we do not think it is a serious holiday; it is only for fun. Dia de los Muertos is not a Mexican version of Halloween. It is based on traditions of the celebration of life and death.

Dia de los Muertos: A Celebration of Life and Memory. This vibrant painting by Diego Rivera beautifully captures the solemn yet festive spirit of honoring the dead—a tradition rich with color, culture, and meaning.

Traditions of Aztec, Toltec, and Others Combined with Christianity

Dia de los Muertos is important in Mexico. People considered mourning for the dead disrespectful; death was a natural phase in life's continuum. The dead were members of the community, kept alive in memory, and may temporarily return to Earth on the Day of the Dead. Pre-Hispanic and Christian feasts joined to take place on the Catholic calendar of All Saints' Day and All Souls' Day.

Morelia

We are heading across farmlands in Central Mexico to Morelia. The Lake Patzcuaro area is best known for its elaborate Day of the Dead celebrations in towns and villages. We were there in December and saw how the cemeteries sparkled. Churches had flowers, especially yellow marigolds.

November 1—Early Morning

First, there is a wake for the little angels to honor children who have died the previous year. Children go to the roofs of neighbors' houses to "steal food." During the day, children run around town "stealing" ears of corn and squash to bring to the community center (usually in the cemetery) to feed everyone. Food is prepared, especially sugar skulls, and the atmosphere is festive. Faces are painted, and the person may have a skeleton-like appearance.

Calavera (Skull) Catrina

In the eighteenth and nineteenth centuries, calavera was a humorous poem that might be put on tombstones and published in papers. The poem made fun of the living. These items became a popular part of the Day of the Dead. Today, you will find clever, biting poems in print, read aloud, and broadcast on television and radio programs.

In the early twentieth century, Posado, a Mexican cartoonist, dressed his personification of death as a skeleton in fancy French garb to mock Mexican society's emulation of Europe. He commented that we are all skeletons underneath the man-made trappings.

In 1947, artist Diego Rivera stylized Posado's skeleton in his mural, "Dream of a Sunday Afternoon in Alameda Park." He dressed the skeleton in a large feminine hat and called her Catrina, a standing term for "the rich." Now, Catrina is the symbol of the Dead, and it is found in restaurants even in the United States. Many of Diego's paintings picture skeletons dressed in fancy clothes, playing instruments, or performing daily tasks.

SMART TIP: While it may seem like Halloween's cousin, the Day of the Dead in Mexico is more than just spooky fun—it's a serious celebration steeped in tradition and festivities.

MEXICO: Dreaming Through Their Eyes—Frida and Diego

No country inspires a more spicy, fiery passion for life than Mexico. It overflows with vibrant art, masterful music, and a complex culture and history. The best-known cultural icons from Mexico are Frida Kahlo and Diego Rivera.

Frida's Home

A fountain springs up, showering two images of coyotes. This place is Coyoacan. Across the road is an azure square stuccoed building that does not look too imposing from the outside. Called Casa Azul, this is where Frida Kahlo was born.

Like many Spanish edifices, the outside does not reveal the character of the inside. We see rooms that reflect Frida's life. As a child, she was stricken with polio. While attending the renowned National Preparatory School in Mexico City, she spied on the famous artist Diego Rivera, who was working on a mural called *The Creation*. This was her first glimpse at her future husband.

One tragic day, the bus she was riding in collided with a street car, ramming a steel rail into her spine and fracturing her pelvis. To entertain her during the gruesome recovery, her parents fitted an easel over her bed, thinking that painting might be a good way to spend time. She took to it like a fish to water. In Casa Azul, we see the infamous orange-backed wheelchair facing a mirror. We could envision Frida in her chair doing one of her famous self-portraits.

When she was eighteen, she reconnected with Diego. Four years later, in 1929, they were married in a civil ceremony by the Mayor of Coyoacan, who proclaimed this merger of two great artists "a historical event." Kahlo was twenty years younger than her groom.

Diego's Home

Traveling by bus, we arrive in a town called Guanajuato. Diego's birthplace is a red stuccoed three-storied apartment. Balconies with lacy iron rails adorn the second and third floors. It is not as visited as Casa Azul and has only a small plaque noting this was the home of painter Diego Rivera.

Diego's father was in the silver mining business. Believing that traditional inhibitions would hinder imagination, his dad cleared a room of everything. At age three, Diego had the run of the room to draw as he wished on the bare walls. He had no interest in what the other kids were playing, but loved plants and nature. At eight, he went to school for the first time. That lasted three months. However, when, at ten, he entered the San Carlos Academy of the Fine Arts, he overwhelmed the instructors.

Today, the museum's ground floor is a re-creation of the Rivera family home. There is an exhibit of his original works. A theater upstairs shows photographs of Frida and Diego.

Diego painted spectacular murals, many of which were controversial in his day but are now regarded as some of Central America's greatest art. One contribution you may see at Mexican restaurants everywhere is Diego's 1924 painting *The Day of the Dead*, in which clothed skeletons play music and dance. The dancing skeletons have become a cultural sensation around the world.

Diego and Frida had an off-and-on marriage. Frida died in 1954, and if you visit her home, you will see her black death mask on her bed with a pink flower-covered and crocheted top, her face surrounded by a green scarf.

After her death, Diego made Casa Azul a museum in memory of Frida. He expanded it with lots of Mexican historical art and artifacts.

SMART TIP: Take a colorful journey through Mexico's artistic legacy by visiting the homes of Frida Kahlo and Diego Rivera. Explore Casa Azul for a glimpse into Frida's world of resilience and self-expression, then wander through Diego's birthplace-turned-museum in Guanajuato, where his bold murals and innovative vision come to life.

FRANCE: Van Gogh—Yellow House and Sunflowers

Of the twenty cities and four countries that Vincent Van Gogh lived in, we visited two places that will be forever emblazoned in our minds: the yellow building with a room upstairs and the cemetery.

From our Seine River cruise, we jump on a bus to Arles, France. We stop at a simple box-style yellow house with no shutters. The address was 2 Place Lamartine, where Vincent had rented four rooms. He had hoped that fellow artist Paul Gauguin would be working with him, but that did not work out. It was in a fit of temper with Gauguin that he cut off his left ear with a razor blade. He bandaged it, wrapped the severed ear in paper, and gave it to a prostitute.

He lived above a huge and unimpressive cafe. We pass through it to go upstairs. The stairs are wooden, with a rickety wooden rail to enable climbing.

Vincent painted *The Yellow Room* in 1888, an interesting time in his life. He was so proud of his work and thought he was achieving his artistic ideals. If you were to go into the room, you would probably ask, as we did, "Why would anyone want to paint this?"

There is a simple wooden twin bed, wooden floors, two cane-bottom chairs with uncomfortable backs, a towel hanging on the door, and six paintings, with the one in the corner skewed. In a letter to his brother Theo, Vincent said he wanted this flattened design to resemble a Japanese print. The walls and door are purple. It is said that this was one of his favorite paintings.

The peek into the bedroom does not take long. We trail back down the rickety stairs and to the bus for another excursion—this time to the village of Auver-sur-Oise. We are set for quite a climb . . . why do people always have to put cemeteries on the top of hills?

The local guide leads us up past a wall that is in one of Van Gogh's paintings. On the left is a small, caramel-colored church with Gothic arched windows and a pointed slanting roof. He described his painting of the church to his brother as violet-hued against a sky of pure cobalt with the windows appearing as blotches.

Van Gogh, shot himself in the chest on July 27, 1890, at age thirty-seven, and died thirty hours later. His grave is covered with green ivy with a few red flowers peeking through. It is not ornate, but a simple stone which reads:

ICI REPOSE
VINCENT VAN GOGH
1853-1890

Here lies a man whose life was one of great angst but also one of unusual talent. He never sold one of his paintings or made any money, but today, his legacy is worth millions.

Being in the places that were part of Van Gogh's life takes on new meaning for us. He was dejected and dismal, but each time we look at one of his paintings like *The Starry Night* or *The Yellow Room*, our souls are touched, and we transcend the Earth.

A Simple Tribute to an Extraordinary Life: The humble tombstones of Vincent Van Gogh and his brother rest side by side—a poignant reminder of the brilliant artist who never sold a painting in his lifetime.

SMART TIP: Inspired by Van Gogh's journey? Take a brush to canvas and unleash your inner artist! Remember, art is not just about perfection; it's about expression. Who knows? You might discover your masterpiece waiting to be unveiled.

EASTER ISLAND:
Beyond the Moai Statues

Marilyn Davis with Evelyn Kelly

Easter Island is tiny; it is only sixty-three square miles in the middle of the Pacific Ocean, and no inhabited island is closer than 1,200 miles. When you stand on one of the island's volcanic peaks and see nothing but ocean, you understand how it got its native name, Rapa Nui, "the navel of the world."

My expectations are low for our visit to "Easter Island," the name given by a Dutchman who "found" the island on Easter Sunday in 1722. However, I am eager to see the famous Moai sculptures, which represent deceased chiefs who could be summoned from their ocean afterlife when the people needed their "mana," their blessings.

The colossal statues are the reason tourists seek out this remote island. These statues have appeared in many pictures and on the cover of an album of the eighties rock band *Styx*.

The mysteries of the Moai are tantalizing, but when I read about Easter Island, it also seems to be an example of ecological failure. The original Polynesian settlers had cut down the last native palm trees around 1400 AD, and a hundred years of commercial sheep grazing by foreign ranchers finished off many other smaller native plants, further eroding the landscape. So, I expect desolation but find the opposite.

Magical Crater

One of the most magical places is the dormant volcano's crater, Rano Kau. One cliff edge has eroded, giving a magnificent window to the Pacific Ocean beyond, and 660 feet below the highest ridge is a lake that has collected fresh rainwater for centuries.

Rano Kau captures my imagination because it seems like a "Garden of Eden" that protects some of the island's original native plants. Missionaries planted grapes there to make wine for mass consumption. Orange trees, figs, pineapples, and medicinal plants are harvested. Only the Rapa Nui people can descend the steep slope, making the garden even more tantalizing.

Forbidden Places

Rapa Nui has many forbidden places. The ahu (altars) that the Moai statues rest on are surrounded by a perimeter of volcanic rock that can't be entered. Unfortunately, these sacred barriers aren't always obvious; for me, one lava rock looks very much like another. One morning, while watching green sea turtles swimming around the legs of bathers, we climb over the rocks facing the ocean, following the turtles. We never look behind us until someone starts yelling at us in Rapa Nui. We understand the anger but not the words until we finally see two huge Moai. We quickly scurry out of the sacred space, but my words of apology in Spanish are lost in the dust and noise of the retreating, angry motorcyclist.

Horses Galore!

The places forbidden to us aren't forbidden to horses. Rapa Nui is estimated to have over 3,000 free-range horses that graze in peoples' gardens, obstruct traffic, eat the flowers in the cemetery, and enter the sacred perimeters of the Moai. When we climb a steep trail in

Rano Raraku to see the sleeping giant sculptures left unfinished in the quarry, I am startled to see a herd of horses on the cliffs above me.

And Dogs, Too

There are no native mammals on Rapa Nui, but besides the horses, it is home to many dogs. I see a couple of dogs politely attending a Catholic mass and others straying into restaurants or lazing in the precincts that are forbidden to us. They always seem well-fed and mild-mannered.

This small island with limited resources always had periods of scarcity when life was challenging. When Europeans first found it, diseases decimated the population, followed in later years by slave raids and abusive treatment by foreign sheep ranchers. The Rapa Nui people somehow survived. Rapa Nui is much more than its famous Moai sculptures; it is a flourishing community with a rich culture and history that isn't just a show for tourists.

SMART TIP: Easter Island, though remote, is accessible via flights from Chile. At the time of this writing, only two small airlines fly into Rama Nui. However, flight availability and airline service can vary, so it's a good idea to check with travel agents or airline websites for the most current information.

USA:
Life on the Lower Mississippi

What would you do if you had no cell phone, radio, or television? Your only entertainment would be what the family could provide. So, if you hear the showboat is coming, you scurry out and sell some eggs to buy a ticket.

Lower Mississippi

We have chosen to go on a River Cruise from New Orleans, Louisiana, to Vicksburg, Mississippi, and back. We are on a paddleboat traveling on this historic river. We could not help but remember the song from the movie *Show Boat* and things that captivated the meaning and history of the Old Man River that keeps rolling along.

Bridge Over Old Man River

We pass under many bridges on our way up the river. In the past, a bridge was a bridge was a bridge. That is, until our guide, who was

A paddleboat adventure is a journey through time, capturing the historical and scenic beauty of the Mississippi River. It showcases iconic Southern architecture of old plantation homes and a romantic and nostalgic river cruise experience.

a civil engineer, enlightened us. There are two bridges named for Louisiana Governor Huey P. Long, who was assassinated in 1935. One of the bridges, the New Orleans bridge, was the first to be built over the Mississippi River. It opened in 1935.

Old Mansions on the River

When you think of the old South, you think of the beautiful antebellum mansions and assume that all Southerners lived on a plantation. Not so; these were the planters' homes (many of them from the North), and only about 3 percent of the population lived in them. They were the major slaveholders—essential to planting crops and taking them to market. There was a large middle class of yeoman farmers, merchants, and professionals who may or may not have had slaves; however, this middle class was important because they provided essential services.

These plantation homes were built in the neoclassical style with columns and are symmetrical. We visited ten of these along the river. Many had fallen into great disrepair but have been restored. Generally, they operate for tours and are available as bed and breakfasts and wedding venues.

Many antebellum homes are in Natchez. It is said that when the Union Army approached, some citizens of Natchez confronted General Grant and said they would surrender without a fight if he agreed not to burn their city or harm their citizens. Not so with Vicksburg. They did not surrender and were bombarded for forty-seven days.

Vicksburg Caves

The military park at Vicksburg is intriguing, but what interests us more is how the people survived. Along the limestone bluffs, the people dug caves that would be their homes for the long siege. In the caves, they set up their living rooms, kitchens, dining rooms, etc. The only problem was that they had to share the cave with snakes. They stayed in the caves until it was time for the Union soldiers to eat. The citizens would go out for light and fresh air and then return to the caves when the shooting began. Those sites have caved in and are not available for visits.

Colorful Characters

The capital of Louisiana is fascinating because it has many colorful characters, including Huey P. Long. This guy set the bar for disreputable politicians. He was hated by the powerful and reviled by others as a dictator. On the other hand, he was loved by the people and considered the champion of the poor. He had a brash personality with no filter of expression, but he got things done: infrastructure, paved roads, university, free schoolbooks, bridges and highways, hospitals, etc. His statue stands before the old Neo-Gothic capitol, now a museum.

The Manchac Swamp

No ending on the Mississippi would be complete without concluding with the bayou, the largest wetland in the United States. This area is where the French Canadians from Acadia settled and are now called Cajuns. Longfellow wrote an epic poem, "Evangeline," set in this area. It is an area of many ghosts, legends, witchcraft, and voodoo.

A local called Aunt Julia was a voodoo priestess and medicine woman who lived in the Manchac swamp. She went around singing this song:

When I die
I take the whole town with me
When I die
I take the whole town

She died on September 19, 1915. Her funeral was held at 4:00 p.m. At the same time, a hurricane hit the town and everyone was killed.

SMART TIP: A river cruise is an easy and comfortable way to see a country. Waterways were the lifeblood of many towns, making them perfect for a scenic journey through history.

PANAMA:
More Than a Canal

We approach Panama City from the air. "Look," Natalie says. "It resembles a combination of Manhattan, Miami Beach, and Las Vegas with a Latin flair."

Yes, and we find that it is indeed such a mixture: a mixture of fascinating history, pirates, a historic canal, beautiful beaches, nearby native populations, and a rainforest with exotic animals.

Fascinating History

In 1519, Pedro Davila founded the first European settlement along the Pacific. Gold from Peru and silver from Bolivia had to be brought from the Pacific across a hazardous forty-seven miles of dense jungle to the Atlantic to send to Spain. This settlement was a target for pirates and home to Dutch, English, and free Black slaves.

One of the first places we are taken to is the ruins of Panama Viejo. Remember, this city is near the Pacific and is the center of transporting Spanish loot. With the blessing of the King of England, Henry Morgan, a privateer, marched 1,400 men from the Atlantic through the dense jungle to burn the settlement. Standing now in memory of this event is a rock tower and ruins of a convent. Henry was reviled in Spain and celebrated in England. He served the rest of his life as a gentlemen farmer in Jamaica. The New Panama City was built a few miles away in 1672.

Panama Canal—One of the Seven Wonders of the Modern World

Cutting a forty-mile waterway connecting the Atlantic to the Pacific should be no problem. After all, Ferdinand de Lesseps designed the Suez Canal, which is 120 miles long. Wrong! This is forty-seven miles of dense jungle with deadly mosquitoes and other critters, and the Pacific waters are much higher than the Atlantic.

We are in the Canal Expansion Observation Center getting ready to go through the Colon Locks, one of the three locks on the canal. There is an air of excitement as we stand in line. What are these locks that will take us from one height to another? We will start our journey from the Caribbean to the Pacific. We are on the ground floor looking out the window. We watch with bright eyes. How did the big ship get into such a narrow canal? Will we hit the sides? No, we watch breathlessly as we slowly emerge. Not a single scrape, but it looks inches away.

Two Nights in the Rainforest

The canal is not the only exciting thing in Panama. We spend two nights at Gamboa Rainforest Resort, with excursions on a real jungle cruise. The howler monkeys do their due diligence and howl all night. What exotic things do you want to see? Three-toed sloths, keel-billed toucans, 1,200 varieties of orchids, the red-eyed tree frog, crocodiles? Yes, we see all of those. We even see the infamous poisonous Panamanian golden frog, known in mythology to bring luck to those who see them. He is a national symbol, pictured on the state lottery tickets. If you are in Panama on August 14, you can help them celebrate National Golden Frog Day.

Native Visits

We are on Gatun Lake, which was created by digging in the canal. On it is a village run by the Embera people. We see their thatched houses on skinny stilts. The ladies have only skirts on and beads, and the men are not wearing much except for a band around the waist and cloth covering their private parts. This is their regular attire; it is not just put on for tourists. Natalie is called to participate in one of their dances; she keeps her attire on, though.

We then visit the Kuna marketplace. Their fabulous handwork is called Mola. It is made of two to seven layers of different colors of cotton cloth sewn together. A design is formed by cutting away parts of each layer. The stitches are so fine they are nearly invisible. We buy two pieces.

The Chicken and the Rooster

We have seen a lot of folk dancers in our travels, but nothing is like these colorful, exotic costumes. The women wear traditional polleras: dresses with various colors and exquisitely patterned designs across the bottom and across the middle. They hold their arms parallel to the floor with the edges of the skirt in their hands. The top that covers their shoulders has the same design, and they wear flowers in their hair. They dance the part of the chickens trying to attract the rooster. A man comes in dressed in brown and red. His boots have special taps to stomp and cavort and catch the eyes of the ladies like a cocky rooster.

SMART TIP: The Panama Canal is an absolute must. Don't overlook the rich history that surrounds this remarkable waterway. Take a moment to delve into the tales of pirates, daring adventurers, and the incredible feat of engineering that brought this canal to life.

CUBA:
A Land Frozen in Time

1959 A young attorney rides victoriously through the streets of Havana. People cheer and flags wave. He has overthrown their current oppressor and promises a better life for all. His name is Fidel Castro. Cuba won its independence from Spain in 1898 with the help of the United States, and since then, it has had relationships with many US companies, such as GE, Frigidaire, and US Sugar.

1959—Cuba becomes frozen in time. Fidel acted swiftly. He took over private property, abolished religion, and killed or imprisoned those who disagreed with him. Professionals and others left the country, and the US started an embargo in 1960.

February 2013—We are among seventeen eager travelers to Cuba with a Friendly Planet People-to-People Educational Tour. We have loaded our suitcases with soap samples, deodorant, and pencils, which are in very short supply in Cuba.

As we land at the Jose Marti International Airport, we have to exchange our money for CUCs; they do not accept American dollars or credit cards at this time. We travel into the city through narrow, bumpy streets with dilapidated buildings held by boards on both sides. We are told that the people do not have money to go to a hardware store to fix their homes. We see bundles of outside electrical wires hanging from poles and several five-decade-old cars on blocks without tires rotting in the heat.

We ride up to the Hilton Hotel; wow, a Hilton, but it has been renamed Habana Libra. You can still see the Hilton logo on the pool floor. The smell of cigar smoke immediately overtakes us. Castro made this hotel his headquarters. Pictures of the Revolutionaries lined the wall with a big sign that states: **1961—The US invaded Cuba. Here, imperialism was defeated in Latin America.**

We travel up the elevator to see Castro's former headquarters, Suite 2354. It later became the Soviet embassy but now caters to dignitaries and tourists.

We are ninety miles from Florida. Many of the people we know are Cubans, but very few know this land. We are in for some adventures.

Arian, Our Cuban Guide

*Arian guides us throughout the trip. At first, she takes us to the "touristy" places: the beautiful plaza that Spain renovated (they completed only one block and then ran out of money), the Bacardi home, and the booksellers market, which is loaded with books about the Castros and Che Guevara. We visit the school where Raul Castro attended and then to the assisted living home to show how the government takes care of its seniors. There, we leave bags of toothpaste, soap, and deodorant.

Arian opens up after spending several days with us. The revolution had broken up her family. Her grandfather opposed Castro and moved to the United States; her mother is a dedicated revolutionary who has guided her thinking. She went to college, majoring in English, and taught school until she became a guide. (At the time of this visit, guides are the highest-paid people in Cuba. Doctors may have to supplement their salaries by driving taxis.)

We are especially interested in going to the ration store. The store is a small kiosk with a few shelves of products, which is different from our huge grocery stores. People receive their weekly coffee, beans, and rice supply. While Arian tries to be positive, she acknowledges many problems—lack of food, black market, inflation, and limited consumer goods.

Old Cars

We spot a 1956 turquoise and white Chevrolet like the one that my husband and I bought in 1956. These cars are exciting until you realize they had been people's cars, which were confiscated. Arian said there would be no parts if the car broke down. Of all Cuban experiences, this one is the most frozen in time.

Arian shows us how the Cuban people are hardy and ingenious. Their amazing art is so colorful and brightens up their lives. One complete street, Fusterlandia, is made of tiles from fallen buildings.

When I buy a piece of swerve art but have nothing to carry it in, I ask if there is a plastic bag. Arian says that these are hard to come by, but the next day, she shows up with a large black garbage bag.

As we leave, we invite her to visit us when she is in the United States. She smiles. We know we will never see her again.

Nothing epitomizes Cuba—a land frozen in time—as the vintage American cars from the 1950s. The cars parked in front of old buildings give a vivid picture of Cuba's cultural and historical landscape.

SMART TIP: Always keep your passport with you. Never give it up. When we arrived at the hotel, we were told to hand over our passports and that the hotel would keep them for our protection, but we did not do it.

* Not the real name of our guide.

PART 6

Love for Fun, Food, Festivities

Take a break from the daily grind.
Escape pressure.
Unwind.
Fun, humorous anecdotes.

Our Love Affair with Toilets of the World

Natalie and I took our first trip abroad in 1993. Little did we know that a mystery would soon be on our hands.

We have arrived in Paris and are staying in a hotel outside of town. As we enter the bathroom, we see two toilets. Seems like a waste of good plumbing.

Later, at the height of frustration, we participate in an informal group discussion on this pressing subject: why the extra toilet in the bathroom? We have a true mystery here. One person says it is for washing clothes. Another says that they sat on the toilet and washed their feet in the little one. A young man—a college student—says that he washed his hair in it. One couple put ice in it and used it to chill their wine. So, we have a mystery on our hands. Although this is the first trip for these travelers, we have studied the travel books and learned the history of the Tower of London and Versailles, but the two toilets stump us.

Timidly and quietly, we ask our local guide why the bathrooms have two toilets. She looks at us like we are escapees from the funny farm. "They are for personal hygiene."

Duh? What does that mean? It is terrible going through Europe knowing that the extra toilet is for personal hygiene but still in the dark. It is not until we get home and do some scholarly research that we find that they are called "bidets."

WCs and Other Strange Beings

We are walking the streets and keep seeing this weird sign: WC. Someone says that it means a water closet, a fancy name for a toilet. Some of these toilets have all kinds of mysterious buttons, chains hanging from the ceiling, or pedals to push. The big problem is that many do not have toilet paper; if they do, you are not supposed to put tissue in the toilet but in a waste can. This is a foreign concept to us. But lesson learned: always carry tissue!

Freeing Your Bladder Is Not Always Free

Before you travel anywhere, it is important to know that toilets may not be free to use. In many places around the world, you have to pay to use the restroom. Some countries have what they call "dragon ladies," who collect money from you and hand you one sheet of toilet tissue.

Just for Men (and Women)

You may find a gender-neutral bathroom. Some share hand-washing facilities; for others, you may find someone of the opposite sex in the next stall. However, there is one positive: the stalls are unlike most American bathrooms with just a divider; most are completely enclosed with a strong door. But when you have to go, it doesn't matter. Get in and get out!

Squat Toilets

These types of toilets are really difficult to learn to develop a love affair with.

We first encounter them in Thailand. One stall has an American toilet seat and a long line of American tourists. Because we are desperate, we choose to experiment with another toilet. We cannot understand why these toilets could be so low with grooves on the seats.

This type of toilet requires one to stand on the lid and squat. The grooves prevent someone from slipping into the toilet. You recognize the ladies who refuse to squat; they have groove marks on the back of their legs. However, we find that it is best in some countries in Asia to forget your Western ways and join the crowd; that is, learn to love these toilets.

Who would not love an adorable hole in the floor? Some even have artistic porcelain places for your feet. Some participants believe these squat toilets are more hygienic than direct contact with a toilet seat and have praised the health benefits of squatting—ask your dog.

Where Can You Find Toilets Like That at Home?

If you cannot develop that love affair with unusual foreign toilets, we suggest looking for stores or restaurants like those at home. Department stores or malls may also have "normal" toilets.

Part of traveling is learning the culture and not trying to make everything like home. Learn that this is part of traveling and develop that love affair with the toilet.

SMART TIP: From these travel adventures, we acclaim the mantra: NEVER LET A GOOD BATHROOM PASS YOU BY, and always bring travel-size tissue.

USA—Upper Mississippi: IS Mark Twain Still Alive?

Mark Twain, as told to Evelyn and Natalie

Hello, my name is Mark Twain (sometimes I am known as Samuel Clements, but I like Twain better). You may always see me wearing my white suit. I like it because it matches my hair and mustache.

I am on a cruise on the Upper Mississippi that begins in Saint Paul, Minnesota, and ends in Saint Louis. I know every inch of this river. You talk about a noble river but then see its humble beginnings above Red Wing, Minnesota. Its origin is a small glacial lake called Itasca; sometimes you can even walk across it.

From these headwaters, it flows south to the Gulf of Mexico. Its elevation at the beginning is 1,475 feet above sea level, dropping to zero feet in the Gulf. More than half the drop occurs in the state of Minnesota.

The spirit of Mark Twain comes alive on a steamship river cruise as we pass lush riverbanks and charming towns along the Mississippi, just as it was in Mark Twain's time.

Why do I tell you this? Because it was my job as a steamboat captain to navigate some of these waters.

River Towns

We will pass from Saint Paul/Minneapolis and Red Wing to Winona, Minnesota, on this cruise. Other towns we pass by are Dubuque, Davenport, Iowa, and Fort Madison before we get to my little hometown of Florida, Missouri, where I came into the world on November 30, 1835. This area was like the frontier, so my family moved to Hannibal when I was five.

Missouri was a slave state, and I spent my summers playing with the kids in the slave community and listening to their stories, tall tales, and spirituals. When I was about eleven, I had bad news and good news. The bad news was that my father died, and I had to quit school; the good news was that I got a job as a printer's apprentice for a local newspaper and could read the news of the world after I completed setting up the type.

My House and Friends

My home in Hannibal was modern for the time. It was a two-story white box house with a white fence like the others in the neighborhood. Now it is a museum. You wonder where I got all my ideas to write my stories. Well, they are all around my house. Do you remember the story of Tom Sawyer and the white-washed fence? Well, that fence borders the property where our house was. I had an adorable sweetheart named Laura Hawkins; she was a role model for Becky Thatcher, a character in my book. There was a guy named Tom Blankenship who lived in an old house; he was the basis of the character of Huckleberry Finn.

And do you want to know of the cave that became the Tom Sawyer cave? It was called MacDougals' Cave, where Tom and Becky met Injun Joe. As a youngster, I was one of the early explorers of this cave that a local man found in 1819. I was always the adventurer, wandering through the deep passages and vaulted chamber using only a candle for light. In *Tom Sawyer*, I tell how a bat swooped down and snuffed out the candle. I mentioned this cave in five books, but Tom Sawyer made it famous.

One of the best books I wrote, often mentioned as a candidate for the Great American novel, was *Adventures of Huckleberry Finn*. The novel explores the topics of race and what it means to be free. I lived at a time when there were great changes in American society. We survived the Civil War and its aftermath. I also traveled West, but came back East.

Mark Twain

How did I get the name Mark Twain? You know that I like writing and have published some stories. But, I had always wanted to be a steamboat pilot. So when the opportunity came, I became an apprentice and got my license in 1859 at twenty-three. I was good and even had my boat for two years. The job as a river pilot was difficult. You have to memorize more than a thousand miles of river bend, water depth, and sunken wrecks in all seasons and stages of the river.

As a pilot, I had to know the calls for safety. When I heard a boatman call out Mark Twain, I knew the river was only two fathoms deep, the minimum for safe navigation. Then came the hateful war in 1861, and the traffic on the river was completely halted. I went west and was working for a newspaper in Virginia City. Some of the articles I wrote were quite funny, so I gave them a humorous author, Mark Twain.

SMART TIP: Review river cruises on the Mississippi River with historians educating travelers on the area. Some have actors impersonating characters, like Mark Twain, for the entire trip.

SOUTH AFRICA:
Dancing with the Zulus

If you have seen the movie *Blended* with Adam Sadler, you have seen the family dancing with Zulus during their vacation to Africa.

We are in Durban, South Africa, a cosmopolitan city on the East Coast of Africa. This diverse city has beautiful unspoiled beaches, and we Floridians are right at home in the pleasant sub-tropical land caressed by warm ocean currents.

Like all cities in South Africa, after apartheid was dismantled, men from different tribes flocked to town to find work. South Africa is the richest country on the African continent, but dark clouds of unemployment, lack of education, and health issues are threatening. In each city, like little children anticipating a parade, lines of men gather along the road, waiting for buses or vans to take them to construction sites. However, we do not see a spirit of despair; the people we speak to have pride in the "New South Africa."

Zululand

The bus leads us to our next adventure: Zululand. Men dressed in loincloths with calves covered with shaggy white wool surround us as we step onto the land of the Zulus. Holding tightly to their spears and shields, the men beckon us to meet a charming young woman who speaks flawless English. Her corona-like crimson hat indicates that she is married. The men and women sing a haunting melody as they escort us along a rocky path through the village.

We move to a large thatched beehive hut. In the meeting hut, a tribal leader presides over the ceremonies. The Zulu dances require a high level of fitness that involves high kicking, clapping, and stamping. The rigorous performance is like no other. The dances of the Zulu tribe transport us into a time when this tribe of strong, fierce warriors conquered surrounding tribes and fought both the Dutch and English.

Then, they calm the dance down and bid us to join them. The lead dancer pulls Natalie out of the crowd to dance with the tribe. They give her a few dance moves and immediately start stamping. Natalie learns quickly. The dance includes a right high kick with a clap under the leg, two right stomps, two left stomps, and a clap. Natalie fits right in.

We are brought back to reality with a large-screen television that runs a video of Shaka-Zulu, the brilliant warrior who brought the nation together into a great military force. Many of us remember a popular television series, *Shaka-Zulu*, set during the Anglo-Zulu War of 1879.

Zulus in the village live in traditional grass-thatched huts called beehives. The natives sleep on the floor. However, our beehive hut is climate-controlled and has fine beds, toilets, running water, and all the comforts of home—but no television. We hear goats wandering around at night and crowing roosters, alarming us that it's time to wake up.

Zulus are renowned weavers of baskets and mats made from palm fronds and other colored grasses. We buy a set of fertility dolls with charming tiny beads, although we do not buy them for permanent use.

Our visit to Zululand captured the essence of Africa. It is one of the most interesting countries for geology, beautiful land formations, culture, and its people.

SMART TIP: When you are on long flights, especially to destinations like South Africa, consider upgrading to first-class or business-class seats for added comfort and amenities. If that's not an option, opt for an aisle seat in coach for easier access to stretch your legs and move around.

SOUTH AFRICA:
Standing on Ostrich Eggs

In Cape Town, South Africa, the famous Table Top Mountain inspired Dutch traders to make it a base for sailing from the East Indies. We ride a cable car up to the top and look over the city. Massive Victorian buildings built by the British still dominate the streets.

This place is so diverse that its inhabitants call it "A World within a City."

Even the Afrikanns' language, also called Cape Dutch, is a mixture of Dutch, German, French, the language of the indigenous Khoisan people, and the dialects of African and Asian slaves in the Dutch colony. British forces seized the Cape Colony in 1795, and thousands came from everywhere in the late nineteenth century to mine for diamonds and gold; this creates an unusual makeup.

Dutch Country

We are leaving Cape Town to drive through a fertile valley where Dutch and French Huguenots found that the soil was perfect for growing grapes and making wine. These estates and the manicured fields are elegant. Stellenbosch, a university town with oak-lined streets, is the center of the proud Afrikaner culture.

This Garden Route leads through native reserves into the green valley of Oudtshoorn. We are now in the ostrich capital of the world, the center of extensive ostrich farms and the ostrich feather industry.

The end of the nineteenth and beginning of the twentieth centuries was an interesting period of history known as the Feather Boom. During this period, one could get more money for one kilogram of ostrich feathers than one kilogram of gold.

Historians call this intriguing group the Ostrich Barons. The barons became extremely wealthy, as fashionable ladies in Europe would never be seen in public without feathers in their hats or boas, made of feathers, around their necks. One baron became so rich that he built a beautiful brownstone mansion called Welgeluk, or Good Luck. However, his luck did not last after World War I. He went bankrupt because he was selling only feathers, and interest in them had waned.

We go to the Safari Ostrich Farm. The owner now diversifies, selling meat, leather, and other products, such as ostrich eggs, for crafts and decoration. One ostrich egg can make the equivalent of twenty-four chicken egg omelets.

Our trip includes visiting the breeding ovens where the large tough eggs hatch into chicks. The owner plops several bone-white, shiny eggs down onto the ground.

"Come, Natalie, stand on the eggs," he says.

She is not sure. Eggs are not generally something that you stand on. We see an egg about six inches long and five inches wide.

"Come on, you can do it!" Everyone cheers her on. She is still not sure.

Though hesitant at first, Natalie stands confidently as she balances on the large Ostrich eggs during a memorable ostrich farm visit—a truly egg-citing moment.

The guide assures her, "Just think: this eggshell is tough. It's about three millimeters thick and is about 96 percent tough calcium carbonate."

She is convinced. Gingerly, she steps up with the help of the guide. She maintains her balance and is now so confident that she can have her picture taken. The eggs do not break!

He says, "Our next task is to ride an ostrich. Who is the first taker?"

Some of the more adventurous ones say, "I'll do it."

Others are reluctant.

But we have no hesitation in skipping this one. Riding an ostrich is not for us.

SMART TIP: When exploring South Africa, don't miss the chance to stand on ostrich eggs at the Safari Ostrich Farm—a truly egg-citing experience! Plus, it makes for a fantastic photo op that's sure to crack a smile.

AUSTRALIA: Rugby, Futbol, and American Football

When we travel, we identify with the favorite sports of the various countries. When in Cuba, we talk baseball. We are in Brazil when the national futbol (soccer) team wins a championship. A guy asks me if I like futbol, and I tell him that I could get into it. The one sport we do have more trouble with is bullfighting in Spain . . . especially when it is the only thing on television.

When Natalie and I are in Australia, New Zealand, and South Africa, we hear everyone talking about rugby and we love their uniforms and striped "rugby" shirts. We know we must find out about it. Our Australian guide invites us to a lounge to watch rugby in Melbourne, Australia. We hear that it is like American football. It starts tame enough. They have a nice big ball similar to an American football, a reasonable field, and the players are lined up on both sides. They huddle differently, though; players on both sides huddle together to start the play. We are a little worried because there are no helmets or pads.

So, with analytical minds, we try to find out what is going on. They are throwing the ball to anyone who can catch it. And when the person has the ball, the other players viciously pile up on him. I think rule number one is to kill the guy with the ball.

What are the Rules?

We ask people around us what the rules are. In between cheers, they give us some guidance for understanding. There are no shoulder pads or helmets; the players are taught to use their arms to make contact. They consider this safer. The ball must be pitched backward to your teammates. There is no blocking to assist the runner. Everyone runs with the ball. You have one second to let go of the ball and purposely fumble when tackled. There are serious repercussions for violations. Players caught disregarding the rules must sit on the bench for a while. Very serious offenses result in a red card, which can mean a suspension for weeks.

We watch an exciting game between an Australian and New Zealand, with Maori natives on the team. In the Maori culture, they have a war dance called the haka, which is used to frighten opponents. The warriors use bulging eyes and poke long tongues in this fierce, threatening stance. At the beginning of the rugby game, the Maori team members line up, look at their opponents with bulging eyes, and waggle their tongues. Who would not be intimidated?

SMART TIP: When in Australia, don't miss the chance to experience the adrenaline-pumping action of rugby. So, grab a pint, don your favorite team's colors, and get ready to cheer your heart out—it's a sporting spectacle you won't want to miss Down Under!

USA: On the Trail with Lewis and Clark

From Seaman's (Lewis's dog) point of view with Evelyn and Natalie

Sometimes, it is good to get a perspective of a great historical event from the eyes of the people who experienced it and a dedicated animal who went all the way. Lewis kept a journal that told Seaman's story, and we share it with you.

Hi, I am Seaman, a great big Newfoundland, weighing about 150 pounds. My breed has lots of hair, with a soft undercoat and a long, silky, black outer coat. I love cold weather and even love to swim in cold water. A guy named Meriwether Lewis bought me for $20. He worked for a very important man, Thomas Jefferson, who bought a huge plot of land from the French. Little did I know what was in store for me.

Seaman, the Newfoundland, played a major role in the success of the Lewis and Clark expedition. His statue with Lewis and Clark reminds us of the adventurous spirit and importance of this rugged journey across the West.

We first went to Fort Wood, Missouri, where I helped load a keelboat with food, maps, books, and useless things like bracelets and medals. You should have seen this keelboat—it had racks and racks underneath, and every inch was packed. For six months, Lewis and his friend Clark studied old maps. They even studied medicine and learned how to bleed people to cure illness and administer a kind of pill called Thunderbolts, which were for purging and cleaning your system.

On May 14, 1804, Lewis, Clark, thirty-one men, and I took off. It was miserable for the men. They had to push the keelboat and two flat-bottomed dugout canoes against the current. Along the river, we met many groups of native peoples. Most were very nice except for one group: the Sioux. I heard they ate dogs; I wanted to avoid them.

New People

November, 1804: It was cold; very cold. We were invited to stay with the Mandan and Hidatsu tribes. Here, something exciting happened. A French Canadian trader named Toussiant Charbonneau joined us. He was an interpreter and cook. But the best part was that his wife was a fourteen-year-old girl named Sacajawea. She soon had a baby boy named Pompey—I called him Pomp. He was my very own to watch over. When we started traveling again in April, they joined us.

One night, when everyone was asleep, I heard a loud crashing sound. It was a huge buffalo charging toward our camp. My voice was loud, so I barked several strong "huffs" and ran him off.

We passed through many rivers, but here really came the challenge. **October 10-17, 1805:** We were on the Snake River and engaged the Nez Perce tribe with some fiddle diplomacy. One of the guys, Crusatte, loved the fiddle, so we all sang and danced—I jumped around. The river rises at the Continental Divide and ends in the deepest river gorge, Hells Canyon. Moving west, we ran into a terrible area with no trees and no firewood for camp. We saw lots of rocks and rapids.

Finally, we left the Snake River. I do want to tell you about an unusual group of natives called the Flatheads. When a child is born, they press the head in a cradle to flatten it.

October 18: We went down the Columbia River to Celilo Falls, met many native chiefs, and gave them trinkets that we had brought. A nice state park will be created someday at the confluence of the Snake and Columbia Rivers named after my dear friend Sacajawea.

We navigated the Dalles, made up of large basalt columns. The Nez Perce tribe left us and warned that some tribes may be hostile. Here, we experienced a new hazard—whirlpools—which were dangerous. We all had to walk along the banks and carry our things; it was treacherous.

November 2: These natives were different from the others. They preferred beads to clothing. Women had two-inch shells in their noses and flattened heads.

Wow! How the wind from the West blows.

We came to the highest falls we have ever seen. Natives named it Multnomah Falls. As photography develops in the future, many photos and selfies will be taken here.

November 3-4: The mornings were very foggy and cold. We were all cold and disagreeable, wrote Master in his diary.

November 9-10: Winds shifted to the southwest and blew violently from the ocean, and then someone said, "Ocean in view." We all rejoiced!

December 8, 1805-March 22, 1806: Our winter quarters are called Fort Clapset, built out of pine and fir trees. We stayed there for 106 days, and it rained every day except twelve. The men's clothes were falling apart, so they caught deer and elk and made clothing and moccasins. Fleas were a problem.

We had traveled 4,142 miles from Saint Louis to the ocean.

March 23, 1806: Hurray! We are going home, but I almost did not make it. Some Chinook natives kidnapped me, but master sent three men to save me.

August 12, 1806: We were moving rapidly going back. They split the party into two groups. Also, Sacajawea and her husband left us here. I missed her and little Pomp.

September 21, 1806: We arrived in Saint Charles, Missouri. Everybody came out to greet us. I was a hero. I got a big steak.

SMART TIP: As you follow the Lewis and Clark trail, come and see me.

USA: Sleepy Hollow Is Not So Sleepy

October in Sleepy Hollow is "the most wonderful time of the year." There are blazing Jack-o-lanterns, exciting street fairs, and yards decorated with a kaleidoscope of reds, greens, and yellows.

We are approaching Sleepy Hollow from Tarrytown, New York. Buried under the black asphalt of Route 9 is the dirt road supposedly traversed by Ichabod Crane and the Headless Horseman, made famous by Washington Irving in the *Legend of Sleepy Hollow*.

We creep along as part of the crowd, haunted by our thoughts of the headless horseman riding past this ghostly oak tree; all of New York must have emptied into this small valley. Despite the mob, we want to find the past in the present and concentrate on the spirit and history of this interesting Dutch colony.

Here Come the Dutch

It all began years ago, in 1609, when the Dutch East India Company hired explorer Henry Hudson, who found a magnificent river and made way for colonies of Dutch people to plant roots in 1658. The settlers were energetic trappers and farmers who pioneered free trade and tolerance. They also brought a wealth of tales, including their ghosts with them. Ghostbusters know the area as one of the most haunted places in the US.

Washington Irving was responsible for the name, Sleepy Hollow; until 1996, it was called North Tarreytown. He moved to the area in

1798 to avoid outbreaks of yellow fever. He was introduced to local ghost stories, including a tale of a Hessian soldier, a mercenary for the British, whose head was shot off by a Continental Army cannon. The moral of the story is not to let superstition guide your actions and overwhelm your reason.

Our guide leads us to the old Dutch church and its churchyard, prominently mentioned in the legend. The headless ghost rides in a nightly quest for his head, hurrying to return to his grave before daybreak. The churchyard is about two and a half acres and is the resting place of settlers like those who inspired Katrina Van Tassel and Brom Bones. However, do not confuse the old church cemetery with the Sleepy Hollow Cemetery.

Sleepy Hollow Cemetery

Sleepy Hollow Cemetery covers about ninety acres and has unique headstones, magnificent mausoleums, twisting narrow roads, and over 45,000 gravesites. Washington Irving is buried here, along with Andrew Carnegie, Walter Chrysler, Elizabeth Arden, Brooke Astor, and William Rockefeller. It is heavily wooded with cedars, sycamores, and oaks.

Even with the crowds, we are alone in our thoughts, reflecting on the names on the tombstones and periodically reminded of these great people. However, seeing the crowds having fun and enjoying themselves is satisfying. We realize that this is not merely a sleepy tourist destination, but a wide-awake land of history and peace; a place of celebration of life and joy.

SMART TIP: While October brings Sleepy Hollow to life with its legendary Halloween festivities, you can visit this charming town at any time of the year. Whether exploring the haunted tales of the Dutch settlers or strolling through the historic Sleepy Hollow Cemetery, there's always something unique in this quaint destination.

SAINT VINCENT: Goat Head Soup, Birthday Party in Saint Vincent

By Casius Pealer III with Evelyn

Casius wrote this email to his parents while he was in the Peace Corps in Saint Vincent (the Leeward Islands in the Caribbean) from 1999 to 2001. They are celebrating a birthday—in a special way.

I woke up at 5:30 a.m., slightly earlier than the usual calls from the dogs and roosters. Today is Paul's birthday, and there will be a big party complete with goat roast later that afternoon. I hear a knock and a loud whisper, "Casius . . . . Casius, wake up. Want to come watch us kill the goat?"

"Graham and two other guys are down by the river. Follow me."

We turn off the road onto a path that turns quickly to dense, high bushes and flowers wet with early morning dew. I can hear Graham giving loud directions to the other two guys in Vincentian dialect, sounding like tribal whoops, indicating the hunt is on.

Vegetation grows even thicker and higher nearest the river. When Paul and I arrive, Graham is downstream under a large tree, holding one end of a rope. A skittish ram goat is at the other end, trying to keep its footing in the shallow riverbed.

Down by the River

Graham, even more so than most Vincentian men, is extremely well-built, with the kind of muscle tone that comes from a life of hard physical work and rice and beans. His dreadlocks are hidden under a Rastafarian cap, and his jeans are rolled up at the legs. He's as comfortable walking barefoot through the river as climbing a coconut tree and wielding the well-worn machete.

The sun is just now coming over the lush mountains behind us, and the body heat from the goat is causing steam to rise in the wet air. The goat's body is across Graham's lap, but he has a hold on one of the horns, forcing it to look away from him as he gently finds his mark with the blade, pulls back, and strikes quickly and true.

Graham and another man tie the hind legs to a tree limb, allowing the blood to drain. They cut around near the hoof of the legs and then straight down, pulling the skin off as they go. They cut around the forelegs and then off over the headless neck, like a wet t-shirt. The muscles and ligaments look disturbingly human without the coarse, dark fur.

The Spectacle Is Over

Paul has begun building a fire. With real work beginning, I feel most comfortable helping Paul. We have trouble getting the still-damp palm fronds to light, and Graham is done cutting before Paul and I start roasting the goat's legs and skull.

Graham soon returns with three dry coconuts. He cuts one up and shares it with me. The others are cut into pieces and placed in the bucket of organs to begin seasoning.

Paul, meanwhile, has gone to the jungle and returns with callaloo leaves, all of which I will later cut up to season the soup with.

Happy Birthday, Paul, with a goat roast.

SMART TIP: If you are on a Caribbean cruise, choose an excursion with the island's history; it is more than beaches and cheap stores.

BRAZIL:
Boat Full of Santas

'Twas the day before Christmas, and all through the town
All the helpers were ready, with never a frown.
The boat was loaded with presents with care
Papai Noel and workers would soon be there.

Yes, we will be Santa or Papai Noel to the children who live on the houseboats on the Amazon River. The director has called all who want to go to climb down into the boat like coming down the chimney. Papai is already in the sleigh (boat), dressed in red with a flowing beard.

We are on Rio Negro, and we plan to visit families who live in houseboats docked along the shore. Many of these communities have lived here for generations. Houseboats are uniquely adapted to the unpredictable rise and fall of the waters. Living in the boats enables them to fish or cultivate small floating gardens. These indigenous families pass down their culture to younger generations, including language, folklore, and traditional skills. Teaching children traditional fishing skills is crucial to their self-sustainability and well-being.

It is Christmas Eve, we join Papai Noel (Santa Claus) to give presents to the children who live in houseboats along the Amazon River. The joy of the children and the excitement of the helpers make this a uniquely festive celebration in the heart of the Amazon.

In Brazil, Santa Claus, known as Papai Noel, comes from the North Pole and distributes gifts to children. On the Amazon River, he slides down the boat ladder instead of the chimney. His sleigh is a boat powered by a motor instead of Donder, Blitzen, and Rudolph.

We are Papai's helpers on our way to deliver joy. Our first stop is at a grey-looking two-room houseboat with a corrugated metal gabled roof. A mother comes out with her daughter. The little girl, who is about seven with long black hair, gets a Barbie doll, and her mom gets a wrapped gift. What joyous smiles!

We move on and wave to a family fishing in a long, narrow boat. Papai hails the group over and hands the children stuffed animals.

The waves are calm. What a great day to be Papai's helper. Next, a nine-year-old boy runs out of the boat house, waving at us and calling for his mother. They are so excited when we hand-wrapped gifts to their family.

The next house is built upon a cliff with stilts. The river is unpredictable, so houses built on the edge of the river must be lifted high. This time, we are greeted beside the river by a very young mother with six children of all ages. They smile when he hands the oldest girl a doll and the others a wrapped gift. We wave goodbye to all.

A mother in a greenhouse invites us to come in, but Papai graciously declines; we still have much to do. Three boys are here, ages three, five, and seven. Their eyes light up when they see that we are giving them soccer balls.

After a few more stops, it is time for Papai and his helpers to eat. We are invited to a family home where they grow their food and make their own medicine. We climb some rather treacherous steps for a meal of their selection: corn, mashed potatoes, and fish. The guide then takes us to their garden, where they raise a variety of tropical fruits such as papaya, and vegetables like corn and potatoes.

Next, we head back down the treacherous stairs to our sleigh to distribute more gifts. We make four more visits and then head back to the North Pole (our ship).

In all of our travels, we have never seen such an act of concern and kindness for those living in an area. We are truly impressed with the gesture of the staff of this tourist boat to share Christmas with others and joy to the ones who have chosen this trip.

And that night . . .

Santa's helpers were all snuggled in their beds
With visions of happy children dancing in their heads.

SMART TIP: Spread some holiday cheer by planning acts of kindness during your travels. Whether it's bringing basic supplies to a community in need or sharing the joy of the season with local families, small gestures can make a big impact.

UNITED ARAB EMIRATES:
Snow Boarding in Dubai

By Jonathan Pait with Natalie

As I step off the gangway of the *USS Essex*, I can't believe my luck. Here I am, a twenty-one-year-old Marine on deployment in Dubai, one of the world's most vibrant and exciting cities. Growing up in a small town in the United States, I could have never imagined that one day I would be exploring foreign lands and experiencing new cultures.

The heat hits me like a wave, the desert sun beating down on my skin as I approach the taxis lined up to take us to our hotel downtown. My two buddies, Zach and Jason, are as excited as I am. We have been working twelve-hour shifts for months, and this three-day port stop is our chance to relax and recharge. While we drive through the city, our driver answers most of our questions about the best places to eat, drink, and experience Dubai like a local.

The buildings are unlike anything I have ever seen: towering skyscrapers that seem to sway in the heat waves. We can't wait to explore this vibrant city. After checking in to our hotel, we head straight to the biggest mall in the world. Our goal: to go skiing indoors in the middle of the desert. I have never snowboarded before but don't want to take a two-hour class, so I confidently tell the staff that I am an expert. The indoor ski slope is massive, with real snow and ski lifts. My friends are already strapping on their gear while I nervously try to figure out how to attach my snowboard to my feet. My fears disappear as soon as we start gliding down the slopes. The adrenaline rush overwhelms me as I glide down the powdery snow. My friend Mateo, who is from New York, has already advanced to hitting jumps and sliding rails. My first few attempts are less than graceful, and my rear end has purple souvenirs.

After two hours on the slopes, we are exhausted and ready to refuel. Our next stop is a fancy rooftop bar, where we indulge in exotic foods and cocktails. I try the Madrooba, a thick, creamy soup with lamb that blows my taste buds away. But the real highlight of the meal is the Luqaimat: small round dumplings that taste like hot fresh donut holes.

Our waitress, Sana, is friendly and eager to hear our stories from back home. We are an interesting mix: Zach is from Alabama, Jason is from Nevada, and I am from Florida. But we bond over our love for adventure and experiencing new things. She tells us about a local concert happening at a nearby nightclub, and we can't resist the opportunity to dance and party with the local "rich and famous." In a secluded area of the city filled with neon lights and cool vibes, we approach a colossal building and head to the forty-third floor. The music is unlike anything I had ever heard, a mix of traditional Arabian sounds blended with modern techno beats.

The next day, we decide to explore more of the city. We visit the iconic Burj Khalifa, the tallest building in the world, and take a camel ride through the desert. We even get lost in the bustling souks, adding to the day's excitement. And through it all, we communicate with locals using a mix of broken Arabic and hand gestures.

Reflecting on that three-day port stop, I realize how lucky I am to have experienced Dubai in all its glory. From skiing indoors, camel rides, and amazing food to dancing the night away with new friends, it was truly an unforgettable experience. It made me realize that traveling isn't just about seeing new places; it's also about meeting amazing people and creating memories that will last a lifetime.

SMART TIP: Don't underestimate the value of local insight when exploring a new destination. Connecting with residents can elevate your travel experience, whether you're finding the best eats, uncovering hidden sites, or diving into the local nightlife scene.

GERMANY: Eating a Hamburger in Hamburg and a Frankfurter in Frankfurt:

Surviving Europe on a Budget

Paul Bebee, as told to Evelyn.
(Evelyn interviewed Paul, who loves to travel and relishes the experience of forming new friendships.)

Paul had always wanted to travel after he finished his schooling, but graduating from college seemed a long way off. However, some surprises come in interesting packages. The mother of Paul's good friend Jim wanted her son to travel to Europe, but not by himself. So she asked Paul to go with him. She would buy the tickets, but they would have to pay for everything else themselves. That sounded like a good deal. So, within three weeks after purchasing the tickets, they were on a flight to London.

They had made no plans except to have fun and experience the world. Their first stop in London was to find lodging accommodations, which they chose at a hostel. A hostel is a lodging alternative for those on a tight budget, normally for younger people. They instantly made new friends. Paul was amazed that people everywhere have one great goal: travel.

Next, journey was to Amsterdam and an inexpensive hostel with accommodations to match. Showers were complete with mold and mildew.

They made friends with Katie, a girl from Germany who invited them to visit her family in Kohn where they stayed in her guest house. These accommodations were slightly different from hostels.

Paul and Jim were outgoing personalities and easily made friends. About twenty young German people gathered to discuss living in the US and Germany. The talk then came to World War II. The grandparents of their new friends had been Nazis, and they talked openly about the Nazi culture. One girl cried when this was mentioned.

A highlight of their trip was eating a hamburger in Hamburg. The hamburgers there were much better than the fast food burgers in America. They were thick and juicy, just like Paul's dad's homemade burgers. Historically, hamburgers originated in Hamburg; however, the idea of making them into sandwiches originated in the United States.

They also decided that eating a hot dog (frankfurter) in Frankfurt would be fun. The frankfurter they found was in between a wiener and bratwurst. Yes, it did originate in Frankfurt when pork sausages similar to hot dogs were invented. The idea of the wiener comes from Vienna, where pork and beef were mixed. Immigrants brought it to the US and made it as a food item to sell on the streets.

Castles and Other Sites

You do not go to Germany without seeing castles and fortresses. Paul was amazed at the Ehrenbreitstein Fortress on the Rhine River, built by the King of Prussia to protect the territory from the French. A youth hostel was in part of this fortress. Paul was impressed that there were still bullet holes from battles in the walls.

Neuengamme concentration camp was touching. This camp and its sub-camps were where millions suffered, died, or were killed. This camp held prisoners of war, gypsies, homosexuals, and those who were physically or mentally handicapped. It was also a death camp.

Paul considered making several new friends one of the true highlights and takeaways from his trip. He keeps in touch with many of them through social media. Although seeing the sites and considering the marvelous heritage was great, the new people and personal side of travel are major memories that can enrich your life.

SMART TIP: If you are on a tight budget, consider bunking up in a hostel for budget-friendly lodging and memorable social encounters.

USA, KEY WEST: A Great Place to Be a Rooster

Hi, my name is Ricardo, and I am a rooster living in Key West, Florida. This is a great place to be a chicken because no one can bother you, and you get to have your picture taken a lot. Everybody says, "Look at that handsome rooster." I don't have to worry about being served as "chicken legs" in a local restaurant.

Don't Touch

We chickens, along with iguanas, are protected species. In Key West, harming or even touching me or my neighbors is prohibited. After all, we are valued members of the community. An ordinance passed in the 1970s protects us against luring, enticing, seizing, molesting, or teasing us. Some say I am the charm of Key West, but others may disagree. You may hear us crowing at all times of the day or night.

I am also a tour guide, taking Natalie and Evelyn through my city to help them understand this unique place. They have never been here before. I start by telling them about our favored son, Jimmy Buffet, who sings "Margaritaville." He is almost as famous as I am.

How Did I Get Here?

Let me answer some of your questions about how my ancestors got here. There are several theories and no general agreement, but most people think that we arrived in the 1860s when people from Cuba moved here during the ten-year civil war on that island.

In addition to being a culinary delight, my ancestors were very important to the economy in another way: sport. The practice was known as cockfighting, and roosters were trained to fight while humans bet on them. This practice was brutal. I am glad it was outlawed in Key West in the late 1970s.

Truman VIP White Glove Experience

I escort Evelyn and Natalie to the Truman White House. Harry Truman, the thirty-third President of the United States, had his Little White House in Key West and spent 175 days here as president. I turn Evelyn and Natalie over to Bob, the expert guide, and then I wait for them. When they finish, I will go with them to this great VIP experience where we will ride around town in the president's limousine. This 1950 president's limousine is a real hit. When the driver sounds the siren, everyone stops and looks when we drive by. People wave and grab their cell phones and cameras to take our pictures. They realize our importance. We wave at them, too.

Dry Tortugas

Evelyn, Natalie, and I go to the Dry Tortugas. I wake them up with my crowing early to get to the airport for a 7:00 a.m. flight on the seaplane. It is easy for me to get on, and I watch as they climb the ladder with no rails, which is not easy for humans. We put on our headphones, strap in, and take

Evelyn is in a seaplane to the Dry Tortugas. She has a panoramic view of turquoise waters and the places where Spanish galleons went down with their cargo of treasures.

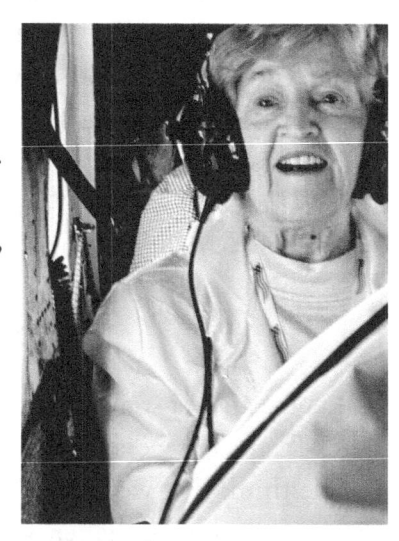

off. We fly over the turquoise water and small islands to the Dry Tortugas. Natalie is in search of Jack Sparrow. I remind her he is a fictional *Pirates of the Caribbean* character.

We land on the beach right at Fort Jefferson. This fort, a national park, was built in 1846 as a USA Military fortress and later was used as a prison for criminals and deserters after the Civil War. Its most famous prisoner was Dr. Samuel Mudd, who was involved in the assassination of President Lincoln.

Upon returning, Natalie says this plane ride was the greatest part: seeing the fort from the air and the remains of the Spanish ship where the diver Melvin Fisher found gold and silver. A ferry can also take you across, but it takes about two and a half to three hours in rather choppy water. Better to stick with the seaplane.

Private Ghost Tour at East Martello and Robert the Doll

I take them to the private ghost tour at East Martello to meet Robert the Doll. This creepy old building was built as a Civil War fortress in 1862, and is supposedly haunted by Civil War soldiers and local citizens who died from yellow fever. You are given an electromagnetic field (EMF) meter to locate ghosts. A ghost must be following Natalie because her EMF indicator lights up.

We are finally going to meet Robert the Doll. Natalie, the adventurer, is asked to go into the dark room first to talk with Robert. She asks questions: How old are you? What is your last name?

He responds by saying "hello" and more words she does not understand. I don't think he answers her questions. The rest of us enter a dark room with a glass encasement and a sheet covering it.

Now, here is his story. On his birthday in 1904, a large life-sized doll was given to Robert Eugene Otto. Otto loved the doll and called it Robert. The doll was given his own room, complete with furniture and toys. As Otto grew, he started blaming Robert for any of the naughty things he had done. Strange things began to happen. Those who possessed the doll had a string of bad luck.

According to the curse, anyone who disrespects Robert will have strange happenings. You must sprinkle holy oil on you to prevent this. Natalie partook of the holy oil; Evelyn did not.

Farewell

I say goodbye to Natalie and Evelyn and wish them well. But if you are ever in Key West, please visit me for a guided tour. You will not have any trouble finding me.

SMART TIP: Ride the less expensive ferry in June, July, or August; in other months, consider taking the seaplane to avoid the rough waters.

PART 7

Cheers to Travel:

Smooth Trips, Smart Tips, and Fun Tricks

Traveling to new and exotic countries is exciting, but navigating the maze of details or not knowing how to start can completely stop adventures. This book takes the hassle out of travel from our experiences and talks with other travelers. You will discover a treasure trove of insights, including exclusive tips never seen in books or blogs. Whether you are a seasoned globetrotter or traveling for the first time, our advice spans the entire spectrum of travel essentials, from mastering the art of packing to unlocking the mysteries of travel hacking. We want you, too, to have a love affair with travel.

For a FREE, up-to-date checklist,
visit our website at travelersatheart.com

From Wish to Bliss

Natalie once was told by a highly educated senator that he wanted to travel overseas but did not know what to do. Natalie asked him the following six questions:

1. What destination do you want to discover: a specific city, country, or attraction? Are you drawn to history, the great outdoors, or perhaps the arts and architecture?
2. Do you have the physical, financial, and time capability to take this adventure?
3. Do you envision traveling solo, with a friend, family, or part of a group?
4. Do you prefer the intimacy of a private tour guide, the camaraderie of a group tour, or the leisurely pace of a cruise or train journey?
5. Will you plan your itinerary or entrust the details to a travel agent?
6. When is the ideal time for your travel?

Like the senator at the Capitol, let us unpack these questions.

Destination Discovery

Are you trying to figure out where you should go on your next adventure? Here are a few things to consider to get you started.

Determine Your Perfect Adventure

Whether you're drawn to the great outdoors, historical landmarks, or big cities, your interests should match your destination. Finding your ideal destination involves research and flexibility.

Research: Books, travel blogs, podcasts, and social media are great ways to discover your destination. But the most powerful resource is word-of-mouth. Ask friends and fellow travelers about their travel experiences and recommendations. Learn about different cultures, religions, and traditions. Research the political landscape and safety precautions using resources like the US State Department website at http://travel.state.gov for travel advisories.

Flexibility: If your destination is not perfect or available, look for other journeys. Seek engaging places beyond the typical tourist circuit. Don't shy away from destinations with complex histories, for which we have coined the term "enlightened travels." Exploring places marked by past hardships can deepen your understanding of humanity and enrich your personal growth and education.

Zip and Zest

Now is the time to determine your physical, financial, and time capability.

Physical Capability: Are you equipped with the necessary physical stamina and health to take on the adventure you seek? Traveling to foreign, especially exotic, lands is not for the faint of heart. Check with your doctor first, then determine the right trip for you. For example, if you have a walking disability, walking to and climbing all of the stairs at Angkor Wat in Cambodia may not be for you. Many countries do not have similar policies toward disabilities like the United States with the Americans with Disabilities Act (ADA).

Financial: Do your current financial resources align with the demands of this journey? Many adventures span from luxurious to economical trips. Traveling is not cheap unless you are backpacking across countries and lodging at hostels. Just remember that the extra expenses—food, excursions, souvenirs, flights, lodging, and a pet sitter, to name a few—add up quickly.

Time: Can you fully commit to engaging in and enjoying this adventure? Know your time constraints. If you have only a week, take advantage of that week and live each moment.

Travel Companions or Going Solo

It's exciting to travel with family or friends. However, if you want to travel and no travel companion is available, do not wait. Travel solo: life is too short to wait.

Solo Traveler: Solo traveling is extremely popular and is growing among single females. Venturing solo provides an opportunity for self-discovery and the acquisition of invaluable life skills.

- **New to globetrotting:** We advise beginning with an organized tour before transitioning to solo journeys.
- **Seasoned travelers:** Take an organized, local tour of the city before venturing alone. This gives you valuable information on what to see and where to go.
- **Focus on solo travelers:** Seek out travel groups tailored for solo adventurers or companies specializing in solo travel experiences.

Family, Friends, and Groups: Choosing your adventure group can make or break a trip. Here's your guide to getting along and selecting the perfect traveling group.

- **Compatible connections:** Whether you're traveling with family or friends, ensuring compatibility is a priority. Discuss expectations, interests, and travel styles beforehand to avoid conflicts. For family travelers, get everyone to participate in the planning of the trip.
- **Communication is key:** Communicate within your group to address concerns, make decisions, and coordinate logistics effectively.
- **Flexibility and compromise:** Remain flexible and open to compromise during your travels. Unexpected challenges will arise. Be prepared.
- **Group dynamics:** Consider the dynamics of your travel group. Do you all want the same itinerary, budget, and activities? A shared vision for the journey enhances the overall experience and minimizes misunderstandings. Small groups may be the best way to travel. We went to India with a company that offered us a private driver and tour guide. This was the best way to see India and understand its culture. Plus, we could deviate from the schedule to spend more time with a silk rug maker or an unscheduled ride on an elephant.
- **Driving decisions:** If your adventure involves road trips, familiarize yourself with local driving laws, insurance requirements, and potential pitfalls. Research age limitations, license validity, and gas payment methods, especially when crossing borders. Read the fine print in rental contracts for hidden clauses to avoid negative surprises. Always ask for a receipt.

Organized Tours, Cruise, or Train

Determining the best type of travel for you can be quite daunting. The following may help you decide which would be most enjoyable for you and your group.

Organized Tours: Whether by bus or river cruise, we highly recommend the experience of stress-free adventures with organized group tours. Let seasoned professionals handle the logistics while you enjoy the ride. Benefits include:

- **Convenience:** Group travel companies take care of every detail, from flights to lodging accommodations to reservations for excursions and restaurants, saving you time and hassle. Most tours are led by knowledgeable tour directors who will guide you through the country and help you with any problems.

- **Skip the lines:** Enjoy line-free entries to attractions, maximizing your time for exploration and relaxation.

- **Structured yet flexible:** While following a set itinerary, group tours also include free time for personal exploration and activities. However, you must comply with strict departure times and luggage pick-up.

- **Peace of mind:** Choose reputable companies with years of experience and built-in emergency escape plans. As exemplified by our experience in Swaziland, having a reputable travel company and a good tour director can mean the difference between being stranded in a country for days due to the president's order to close the border or safely returning home immediately.

Cruise Advantages: Set sail for adventure with the following perks of cruising:

- **All-inclusive luxury:** Indulge in all-inclusive amenities, from gourmet dining to onboard entertainment.
- **Unpacking once:** Explore multiple destinations in one trip, with the convenience of unpacking only once.
- **Onboard activities:** Enjoy many onboard activities, from spa treatments to Broadway-style shows, catering to every taste and preference.
- **Scenic views:** Enjoy breathtaking ocean vistas and stunning port cities, offering beautiful photo opportunities.
- **Inland excursion:** For a more exhilarating experience, some cruises offer inland tours. While our Alaska cruise was special, we will never forget our experience taking an overland excursion to Dawson City, Yukon.

Train Travel Perks: Embark on a scenic journey aboard a train and enjoy the following advantages:

- **Scenic routes:** Picturesque landscapes and charming countryside views offer each destination a unique perspective. Try a glass-dome train that gives panoramic, scenic views.
- **Relaxing atmosphere:** Enjoy the comfort and relaxation of train travel with spacious seating and the freedom to move around at your leisure.
- **Eco-friendly option:** This option for eco-friendly transportation reduces your carbon footprint while exploring the world.

DIY Adventures vs. Travel Agent Journeys

Whether you are taking a solo journey or seeking the expertise of a seasoned agent, weigh the pros and cons and choose the option that best suits your travel style and preferences.

Making Your Plans: Making your plans requires thorough research, organization, and time.

- **Flights:** Once you are confident in your direction of the six-question exercise and have methodically researched your destination, start scouring travel search engines for flights. Don't settle for the first offer—rates fluctuate daily. Opt for mid-week flights and consider budget airlines, but beware of additional fees. Know your layover time between connections. You may not make your flight if the connecting flight layover is less than two hours. Sign up for travel deal websites and airline newsletters to stay in the loop and compare prices across booking sites while watching for seasonal price increases.

- **Seats:** Booking early is key for the best prices and seat selection. We like seats closer to the front. It's easier for boarding and disembarking. If sitting in coach, secure a bulkhead if you need more room or an aisle seat if you treasure quicker trips to the bathroom. To avoid motion sickness, sit in an aisle seat and in front of the wings for maximum stability on flight. Also, carry your motion sickness medicine.

- **Boats and trains:** Book in advance, especially for popular cruises. There are numerous cruise lines and destinations. Determine the cruise that best suits your desires. Don't forget your passport; you will need it to get on the ship, even if you do not plan to leave the ship.

- **Lodging accommodations:** Book early and know the purpose of the hotel. If it is a resort or casino, fees may be included.
- **Secure Show Tickets and Reservations in Advance:** Don't wait until you are there to secure your reservation. It may be completely booked if it is a popular restaurant or show.

Travel Agent Advantage: While some may prefer the thrill of creating their itinerary, we prefer the expertise and convenience a trusted travel agent offers. By enlisting the help of a knowledgeable agent, you gain access to insider tips and personalized recommendations tailored to your preferences. From navigating visa requirements to securing the best deals on accommodations, a reputable agent can handle all details, ensuring a stress-free and seamless travel experience.

Timing Your Travels

The art of picking the perfect moment takes research.

Weather: Before setting off on your next adventure, consider climate, seasonal variations, and potentially extreme weather conditions.

Local Calendar: Familiarize yourself with the destination's calendar, including festivals, religious events, sports competitions, animal migrations, and local school holidays. Timing your trip to coincide with these events can enhance your experience and provide unique cultural insights. We timed our visit to Rio de Janeiro during their national football game. Argentina won, and it was spectacular to watch all of the people celebrating under a shower of fireworks framing the Christ Redeemer statue.

Tourist Season: Beware of peak tourist seasons, which often mean crowded attractions and higher prices.

Pre-Travel Checklist

Before you head out, ensure that you are prepared to avoid any headaches or snags.

A Few Months Out: By now, you should have your travel plans solidified and travel accommodations booked. You are a few months away from your adventure. What should you do?

Stay connected: Give your loved ones advance notice of your travel plans. Schedule accommodations in advance if you have someone that will be caring for your home or animals while you are away. We created a notebook called "In Case of Emergency" that organizes important information and documents. Make copies of your passport, driver's license, and TSA PreCheck/Global Entry, and don't forget to leave the information about your trip, including the location of hotels, flights, etc.

Passport: Apply for a passport six months before traveling to a foreign country, or ensure your current passport is valid for at least six months before expiration. Check for at least two blank pages for new stamps.

Visa: Contact a travel agent or booking company to confirm visa requirements, or if conducting your own research, communicate directly with the country's embassies or consulates. Always travel within the dates required and PRINT a hard copy of your visa. A friend flew to India and had to return because India's immigration would not accept her. Her visa was two days later than identified, and she did not print the original visa acceptance notification.

Travel insurance: Invest in travel insurance to safeguard against unforeseen events like flight cancellations or medical emergencies. We planned an excursion flight to the Arctic Circle. Natalie got very ill the day before the flight, and we canceled the excursion. Because of her travel insurance, she received a full refund.

TSA Pre-Check or Global Entry: To prevent standing in long lines at airport security, apply for TSA Pre-Check or Global Entry in advance. Applying for an interview takes effort and time, but it is well worth it!

Body Boost: Get your body in shape for the adventure ahead with a fitness regimen. Start a walking plan and drink fluids daily. Get a checkup from your doctor or visit a travel nurse at your health department for required vaccinations.

Pet Preparations: Prioritize the well-being of your furry companions by arranging for a dependable pet sitter or suitable lodging. Compile information on your furry companion, including health records, vaccinations, food intake, and special needs.

Language Essentials: Learn key phrases in the local language or download a translator app to navigate effectively. Key phrases include: Hello, how are you? Where are the toilets? How much? Please. Thank you. Goodbye.

Power Up: Research voltage converter to connect to the country's electrical outlet. Your converter must include various ports to charge all of your electronics.

Days Away
First Steps

With just a few days until takeoff, dive into this section dedicated to last-minute preparations.

Important Information: Make four copies of your essential documents, including your passport, visa, and trip details. Place one set in your "In Case of Emergency" notebook for safekeeping and the others in your carry-ons. Don't forget to snap photos of these vital papers and store them digitally on your phone and laptop.

Contacts: We create a small list of family and friends, credit card contacts, and embassy or consulate. We put it in our carry-on.

Prescriptions: Stock up on necessary prescriptions, with an extra seven days' worth to cover any unexpected delays. List medications, including dosage and generic names, and include them with your contact list.

Cell Phone: Mobile networks differ from country to country. Check with your provider to see if your wireless plan will work in your destination. Consider an international plan to avoid roaming charges. Utilize local SIM packages or download free Wi-Fi apps. Using the phone in your hotel room is very expensive.

Weather: Check the latest weather forecasts at your destination and pack your bags accordingly. Arm yourself with a mini folding umbrella and lightweight, water-resistant jacket.

Be in the Know: Enroll in "Smart Traveler's Enrollment Program (STEP)" for text alerts.

Currency Conundrum

Here we will dive into the intricacies of managing currencies, ensuring you are knowledgeable about handling financial challenges.

Withdraw Cash: We recommend carrying a variety of denominations, including at least a few dozen one dollar bills. It is very important to ask for brand-new, crisp bills. Many countries will not accept bills that are crumpled or marked. This provides flexibility for tipping taxi drivers, bellmen, and other services.

Hideaway Money: To mitigate the risk of loss, divide your cash into three locations. We keep enough money for the day in our handbags and stash the rest in the hotel safe or in a locked suitcase.

Credit Cards and Debit Cards: Bring two credit cards for your travels. Before your trip, verify with your credit card issuer that your cards are travel-friendly. Another reason to notify them of your plans is to avoid potential disruptions due to fraud prevention measures, which may lead to transactions being blocked. Opt for no-fee bank cards whenever possible. Look for cards that waive foreign transaction fees and ATM fees to avoid unnecessary charges while abroad. If your credit card goes missing, immediately call the company and lock or cancel your card. We use airline credit cards to increase points for free seat upgrades. When using debit cards, keep enough money in your account specifically for the trip.

Exchanging Money: You should exchange a small amount of cash before or when you arrive. There may be instances where only local cash is accepted, such as a coffee shop or when entering the "toilets." We gradually exchange cash for local currency at various banks. Never exchange cash on the street. Remember, if you're left with a hefty sum of foreign cash post-trip, the return rate might not be in your favor, so exchange wisely!

ATMs: When using ATMs abroad, remember to withdraw the local currency and memorize your PIN.

Keep Receipts: Keep receipts and write the purchase on them. Put them securely in your luggage for safekeeping because you never know when you'll need proof of purchase.

Pack Like a Pro

Safeguarding Luggage: First, look at ways to safeguard your luggage. Take the following preemptive measures to mitigate the chaos if your bags go astray.

- **Photo of luggage:** Take photos of your carry-on and check-in luggage. Personalize your luggage with unique tags or markings, ensuring it stands out in a sea of suitcases.
- **Hide personal information:** Do not display your address for everyone to see. Instead, include your email address on your outer luggage tag and keep your home address inside the luggage.
- **Travel locks and bands:** Remember to secure your bags with TSA-approved locks, which add an extra layer of protection. We also secure our check-in luggage with locked bands around the bag. This gives you the peace of mind of knowing that your luggage will not open unexpectedly.
- **Tracking:** Secure your luggage with Air Tags for constant surveillance.
- **Lodging identification:** We arm our check-in suitcase with the location of our next lodging destination to ensure that our luggage will make it there, even if we don't.

Suitcase Strategies: Whether jet-setting to a tropical paradise or braving the frosty embrace of winter, selecting the right suitcase is an art form.
- **Size (and weight) matters:** Many airlines have implemented strict size limits on carry-on bags and weight limits for check-ins. Research airline requirements of bag dimensions and weight restrictions. If your carry-on is too large, you may have to check your luggage for an extra fee. An extra fee will also be charged if your luggage exceeds the weight limit. We were behind a traveler at the check-in counter who opened his bag and pulled out his underwear and other personal unmentionables to meet the weight limit. Some travelers buy a luggage scale; we just use our own bathroom scales. At least we are putting our scales to good use.

Handbags and Wallets: Choosing the right gear is important as you travel, and this is especially true for the items you will be lugging around as you explore. Here are a few tips to consider as you pack these items.

- **Size:** It's wise to bring a compact, convenient cross-body shoulder handbag. Many museums enforce stringent bag size restrictions for security reasons, barring entry to backpacks, carry-on bags, or oversized purses.
- **Essentials:** Stash passport, visa, government identification, Global Entry, credit cards, cash, and other forms of payment in a travel wallet with RFID blocking protection.
- **Cell:** Place your cell phone in a specific, go-to pocket so you know exactly where it is.
- **Must-haves:** Remember your reading glasses, sunglasses, pocket umbrella, keys, and travel packet of tissues. Yes, you heard us. You will thank us when faced with a restroom devoid of toilet paper.
- **Wallet:** When safeguarding your wallet, heed this golden rule: never tuck your wallet into your back pocket, lest you become an unwitting target for pickpockets prowling the streets. Instead, opt for a slim, sleek wallet that fits snugly into your front or zipped pockets. Bulging wallets must go; leave all cards not necessary for your trip at home.

Inside the Carry-On: Inside the important carry-on bag includes the following, plus your toiletry bag and medicine kit:

- **Documents:** Store important travel documents such as tickets, travel insurance, and itineraries in waterproof envelopes.

- **Clothes:** Pack one change of clothes and undergarments just in case your luggage ends up in Timbuktu.
- **Electronics:** This includes your laptop, tablet, electronic chargers, headphones or earbuds, and power cords.
- **Water bottle:** Bring an empty bottle to fill up post-security to keep hydrated.
- **Go-to bag:** We have a small bag that can be quickly removed from the carry-on bag with items that will create a comfortable sanctuary for our flight: mask, lip balm, face mist, antibacterial wipes, and sealed snacks.

Toiletry Bag: Make sure that you have everything you need to keep yourself fresh during your travels.

- **Essentials:** Ensure your bag is stocked with essential, travel-size or sample-size containers of moisturizer, toothpaste, toothbrush, deodorant, hairspray, razor, brush, and comb.
- **Perfume/cologne:** Learn from the cautionary tale of our friend, who suffered the consequences of a broken high-end cologne bottle that left an overpowering scent lingering throughout the journey. Our recommendation is not to wear perfume/cologne.

Medicine Kit: If traveling with companions, consider pooling your resources and creating a super-sized kit for the entire group. Here are the essentials for your medicine kit: prescriptions, aspirin, painkillers, cold/flu medicine, sleep aid, and medications to deal with stomach, altitude, or motion sickness. Prepare for allergies and indigestion with antacids and allergy medication. Equip yourself with anti-itch cream, antibiotics, sunscreen, and ointments.

Building the Perfect Travel Wardrobe

As travelers who pride ourselves on our packing prowess, even the most adept adventurers can overpack. Remember, you're not running for a beauty contest. Here are tips on how to travel light and determine what to wear with our Three Stage Packing approach:

Stage One: Start early by laying out your clothes. Consider your destination's weather, season, activities, and cultural standards. Your travel clothes should be comfortable, light, and last weeks without washing while still feeling and smelling brand new. We look for five qualities in travel clothes:

1. Easy care and packs small
2. Regulates temperature that stays cool when it's warm and warm when it's cool
3. Keeps moisture away from you
4. Prevents odor
5. Wrinkle-resistant

Stage Two: Remove any clothing you're not 100 percent sure about.

Stage Three: Our goal is to wear everything at least twice. Here are two outfit ideas: 1. Mix and match outfits. 2. Focus on a color scheme, such as black and white with a splash of color with a scarf. When traveling for more than a week, we pack two pairs of pants and shirts, one change of clothes in the carry-on, and wear a set. Therefore, we bring four pairs of pants and shirts. We mix and match clothes; it looks like we wear a new outfit every day.

Twelve Key Packing Perfections

Finally, you pick out the clothes you are bringing. Let's follow the twelve key packing ideas:

1. Packing Cubes: The first step is organization. Roll similar clothing items into a cube. We pack pants into one cube and shirts in another, while undergarments enjoy smaller cubes. We have another cube for scarves, socks, etc.

2. Jewelry: Do not bring expensive jewelry. However, if you can't go without jewelry, pack custom jewelry. It won't be the end of the world if you lose it.

3. Dress Culturally Appropriate: Some countries have specific laws or rules about appropriate clothing, so make sure you check this before you start packing and choose your outfits accordingly. This also helps you avoid drawing attention to yourself. Want to catch the attention of every pickpocket in Paris? Show up in shorts, tennis shoes, and a T-shirt. For extra credit, wear a shirt featuring your favorite university.

4. Undergarments: We pack old undergarments and throw them away after use. This limits our dirty clothes and purges old undergarments from our drawers.

5. Jacket: Wear your jacket on the flight to save luggage space. Some sites do not allow umbrellas; therefore, always bring a rain-repellent jacket.

6. Cover Up or Wrap: Always have a wrap with you. It can cover the shoulders or be worn when entering religious places. We use our wrap as an extra cover on cold planes or roll it up to use as a pillow.

7. Appropriate Shoes: Bring two or three pairs of shoes. Closed-toe shoes are preferable, but sometimes cute sandals will make your day. Do not bring high heels or a new pair of shoes to wear for the first time. If you do, make sure to bring lots of bandages.

8. Staying Clean and Fresh: Bring dryer sheets to keep your clothes smelling fresh. Plus, they are very good mosquito repellants. We tuck away a washcloth in a plastic bag; a simple luxury, but more and more hotels are charging for a washcloth. If we have at least two days in the same hotel, we use our bathroom sink as a washing machine and use detergent sheets to wash clothes. Learn this handy tip for a fast way to dry clothes: Wring water out of clothes, lay your clothes on a towel and fold it over the clothes, and finally wring the towel with your clothes inside. This eliminates additional moisture. Hang the items on a portable clothesline or towel racks.

9. Water and Sodas: We stash small sodas and water bottles in zip-locked bags within our check-in luggage, ensuring we are never without water or our preferred soft drink.

10. Secondary Bag: This bag is for items like hairspray, a travel clock, travel locks, a small umbrella, etc.

11. Heavy Bottom: Place heavier items at the bottom of your bag and layer clothing on top to maximize space.

12. Do Nots: Valuable items, such as prescriptions, cameras, chargers, laptops, passports, jewelry, etc., should not be packed in your check-in luggage.

Are We There Yet?

So, are you packed and psyched for your journey? Grab your gear, and let's go!

Traveling to Departure Point: The journey to the skies, rails, or seas is an adventure in itself, and how you travel to your departure point can set the tone for the entire expedition.

- **Your vehicle:** Give yourself plenty of time to drive to the airport and find parking. If you're seeking an alternative to parking at the port, consider taking advantage of hotel parking packages. With these packages, you can utilize parking only or enjoy free parking and a cozy night's stay before or after your flight. With the hotel shuttle at your service, you'll be easily shuttled to and from the airport, ensuring a seamless transition from land to air.

- **Chauffeur:** If you're craving the royal treatment, why not indulge in the luxury of a driving service? They'll whisk you away from your doorstep, carefully handle your bags, and deliver you to the port. Sure, it may come with a heftier price tag, but the convenience is worth its weight in gold.
- **Rental:** If you rent a car, check the type of fuel required to avoid unexpected or long pit stops along the way. Read the manual (yes, really). We check the wipers, lights, cruise control, mirrors and connect electronics with the car before getting on the road. Fuel up before returning.

Airport: Ready, Set, Board

Between waiting in line at security and rushing to your gate before the doors close, flying can be a stressful experience. Get ready to navigate the pre-flight hustle and bustle with finesse.

Print Ticket: Most seasoned flyers use their airline app to get an electronic boarding pass. We print our boarding pass as insurance in case our electronic boarding pass is unavailable.

Arrive Early: For domestic flights, arrive two hours before BOARDING time and three hours for international flights.

Stay Connected: Download airline apps for flight updates. Confirm and check in within twenty-four hours before the flight with your app. Unless you have check-in luggage, you can bypass long lines at the check-in desk and go straight to security.

Airport Check-In: You will need your airline confirmation or ticket number and passport/identification.

Disabilities: Contact your carrier to inform them about your disability in advance. They will have a wheelchair and staff ready to walk you through security and the long corridors of airport gates. This is extremely helpful for those who cannot maintain their balance on escalators. Don't forget to tip the one who helps.

Security: Consider enrolling in TSA PreCheck (within the US) or Global Entry (international) for expedited screening and shorter lines. Don't be that person holding up security to empty your pockets. Do this while you are waiting in the security line. Fasten all bag closures to ensure your items do not fall out while being scanned. We do not wear jewelry, belts, or anything else to the airport that may be metal to alert security. We also wear shoes that are easy to slip off and slip back on without shoelaces. Never leave the security area without checking for all your belongings.

On Your Way to the Gate: Check the flight schedule board for any gate changes to avoid unnecessary delays. For frequent travelers, airport lounges offer a serene escape with complimentary amenities.

Pay Attention: Pay attention to boarding times. Too many tourists miss their flights because they don't pay attention to the times and are too engaged in a conversation or book.

Seven Ways to Make Flying Fun

Treat your flight like a cozy evening at home by envisioning yourself lounging on your couch in front of your television.

1. Create a Serene Environment: Stow your carry-on under the seat in front of you to keep your essentials in reach. Establish a soothing routine with meditation, music, or movies from the airline's selection or your own downloaded content.

2. Comfortable Clothes: The last thing you want is to feel uncomfortable in tight pants for a fourteen-hour flight. Wear comfortable, loose clothes.

3. Good Health: We use the S.A.M. approach to long flights. S=socks, wear compression socks to prevent blood clots; A=agua, drink plenty of water to keep hydrated; M=move, get up and walk around every two hours. We also like to hydrate our skin by constantly applying a light moisturizer.

4. Jet Lag: As soon as you board the plane, adjust your watch to the time of your destination. An experienced international traveler gave us the tip of taking a sleep aid thirty minutes following your first meal during an overnight journey. Then, block out the light with an eye mask.

5. Bathroom: The puddle on the bathroom floor is not water. Always wear shoes when attending the bathroom.

6. Landing: When your flight is ready to touch down, open your mouth wide to help elevate the pressure and clear your ears. Learn disembarkment etiquette—when leaving the plane, always wait for those in front of you to leave first.

Hotel Hacks

These hotel hacks will elevate your experience and provide peace of mind throughout your stay.

Hotel Membership: Maximize your benefits as a frequent traveler by considering a hotel credit card or rewards program to earn points for free stays. Remember to have your rewards number available and ensure it counts toward your stay. Always ask for upgrades when checking in. If the hotel is not full, they may accommodate you.

Safe Stay: Check all windows and sliding doors to ensure they are locked. We double-check our door closure to ensure it is locked when we leave the room. Consider bringing a portable door lock or door stopper for added security inside your room, especially when traveling solo. Most importantly, luggage should be locked. Use the safe in the hotel room to store valuables.

Prepare for Emergencies: Always have a robe or coat and shoes ready to grab immediately in case of an emergency. We learned this from firsthand experience. When staying in Dawson City, Yukon, the fire alarm went off in the middle of the night and we all poured out into the cold street, not wearing appropriate clothes.

13 Things to Know when Traveling to other Countries

Travel forces you to get out of your comfort zone. Here are some valuable tips to get the most out of your traveling experience in another country:

1. Be on Your Best Behavior

Americans have a reputation for being loud and clueless about the customs of countries they visit. Help dispel this assumption by behaving in a way that puts you and all of us in a positive light.

Exercise Patience: Embrace patience and tolerance, especially when faced with cultural differences or language barriers.

Respect Locals: Whether you are capturing memories with your camera or haggling in a marketplace for the perfect scarf, respect those who call this country their home. Remember you're a guest in their country; courteous behavior goes a long way.

Adapt to Differences: Understand that the rights and norms you are accustomed to may not apply in other countries. Know and adapt to local customs and laws accordingly. Embrace cultural differences and learn about their history, culture, and way of life.

Avoid Attention: Keep a low profile and avoid drawing unnecessary attention to yourself.

2. Snapping Photos
Know local regulations. Avoid photographing law enforcement, border patrol, or sensitive areas like holy sites or inside museums.

3. Know How to Find Your Way Back
To help you find your way back, take photos of your bus, hotel, site, and parking lot, as well as street signs or other distinguishable markers. Also make sure to take your hotel's business card and/or room card when you leave so you know your lodging location.

4. Safety on the Street
Walking the streets of a new city allows you to explore off-the-beaten-path areas. However, be aware of a multitude of concerns. First, foreign streets are very uneven, and if there are sidewalks, they may be crowded with local vendors or bikes. Falls are prevalent among travelers.

Research local scams and cunning tactics of criminals targeting travelers. Beware of pickpockets, and walk with your handbag away from the curb to avoid drive-by snatchers.

Distraction can make us vulnerable. In Romania, a gypsy hit Evelyn's souvenir purchase, trying to distract her in order to grab her handbag. She knew their trick and yelled, "No." They ran away.

Never hang your bag over the back of your chair or leave it unattended, even in a hotel lobby.

5. Nothing is Free
Never take or accept an item that does not belong to you, even if offered.

6. Transportation
Utilize their mass transit system when available. When using a ride sharing service, verify the driver's identity. Avoid the local who offers a ride in their vehicle.

7. Meals and Food Safety
Experiencing local cuisines will enhance your visit. Go to a grocery store to learn about the local foods and diets.

Travel bloggers encourage eating street food to avoid missing out on culture. But beware of the consequences. We recommend experiencing reputable restaurants or those recommended by your travel guide. If you cannot resist that fajita from a street vendor, make sure you bring your stomach medicine. Avoid pre-cut salads or fruits unless cleaned with purified water. Be leery of raw foods; pre-heated rice and meat are risky. Finally, never leave your drink unattended. If it doesn't taste right, don't drink it.

8. Water Restrictions
Drinking tap water is never recommended. We open our own purchased bottled water. If a server has opened the cap, we will not accept it. Never use ice in your drink, even in high-end hotels or restaurants. And remember, use bottled water when brushing your teeth. Montezuma's Revenge is real.

9. Public Bathrooms

Do not use public restrooms. Instead, go to familiar territory, like a food chain or coffee shop you frequent back home. You will have to buy something, but in return, the restrooms are cleaner.

10. Secure Wi-Fi

Be careful of public Wi-Fi. Hackers can access your data and steal valuable information, including credit card or social security numbers. Secure your connections by setting up a virtual private network (VPN) that will allow you to access the internet covertly. Never plug your USB cord directly into the port at an airport or hotel. Bring a data scrambler that connects your cord to the USB port.

11. Social Media Caution

Be careful when posting your holiday photos on social media. Do not post about your travels until you return home to avoid potential security risks.

12. Souvenirs

Look for locally made products to support the country's economy. Shop at local department stores for more affordable and less "touristy" souvenirs. Avoid purchasing souvenirs made from animal parts to prevent contributing to the illegal wildlife trade and potential legal trouble.

13. Adventure Safety

Safety inspections and regulations vary between countries. Therefore, be careful when using zip lines, hanging bridges, etc. Prioritize safety when interacting with wildlife by checking the reputation and reliability of animal operators.

Conclusion

Armed with newfound insights and a deeper appreciation for the differences in our world, may we continue to navigate foreign lands with reverence, humility, and an open heart. Let us embrace each encounter as an opportunity to grow, connect, and celebrate the human experience. As we say goodbye to one adventure, let us eagerly anticipate the next journey. May your adventures bring you closer to having a love affair with traveling, and allow traveling to be your ticket to an exhilarating life!

Acknowledgments

We are so grateful to our many friends who encouraged us to write this book. It came about as we started telling stories about what happened to us on our travels to all continents, eighty-eight countries, and all fifty states. Many have added to our stories, and others have inspired us to write about our experiences.

Our eternal thanks to the first (beta) readers who volunteered to read 102 stories and who gave us valuable feedback. We will be ever grateful to: Dr. Christine Caulfield, Daniel Dean, Alexa Harvey, Margery Howard, Patricia Nevard, Dr. Casius Pealer II, Gwynn Pealer, Diane Schrier, and Rich Hautanen.

We thank Marilyn Davis, Jonathan Tait, and Casius Pealer III for writing meaningful travel stories of their own experiences.

We appreciate those who had marvelous stories to tell and let us interview them: Paul Bebee, Valerie Gladhill, Margery Howard, and Dr. Donna Robinson.

Thank you to Senior Learners Inc. at the College of Central Florida and Master the Possibilities at On Top of the World, Ocala, Florida, for inviting Evelyn to present "Armchair Adventures" about our travels over the past several years.

We especially appreciate our travel agent, April Powell from Ocala Travel, who helped us through the years and continue to assist us on our journey to become seasoned travelers.

Special thanks to Sharlene Kelly Chatham who helped us read the manuscript and encouraged us along the way.

We also thank and appreciate the Get Published Now (GPN) staff and our dear coach, Mary Lou Reid, Editor Valerie Costa, Cristina Smith, Geoffrey Berwind, Steve Harrison, Christy Day, and others.

When Evelyn submitted a travel article to *Life Styles Over 50*, the editor, Michelle Baker, said, "Write something that only you can write." That gave us the idea of the adventures we have experienced. Thank you, Michelle, for this perspective and for publishing "Armchair Adventures" each month.

Disclaimer: The stories and travel tips are our own experiences or those that were told to us with their permission.

About the Authors

Evelyn Kelly, a resident of Ocala, Florida, is a writer, speaker, and teacher. She holds a Ph.D. from the University of Florida, a master's degree in religion, and a Bachelor of Arts degree from the University of Tennessee. Her education and interests are diverse. Her undergraduate studies included microbiology, English, and history. Evelyn has written twenty-two books on such topics as stem cells and a two-volume encyclopedia of genetics. Evelyn has taught at four universities. She speaks and writes on travel topics, including a popular series called "Armchair Adventures."

Natalie Kelly is an accomplished writer and the Chief Executive Officer of a prominent state organization, residing in Tallahassee, Florida. She holds a Master of Science in Communications and a Bachelor of Science in Visual Arts, with a concentration in Art and Art History, from The Florida State University.

With a distinguished career spanning over thirty-five years in government affairs at the state and national levels, Natalie has held several notable positions, including serving as the youngest female staff director in the Florida Senate and as a director in Washington, D.C. She was the owner of a successful public relations and lobbying firm.

In addition to her executive leadership, Natalie contributes op-eds to various newspapers and is a sought-after speaker on a wide range of topics. Her expertise and insights continue to influence and inspire audiences across different platforms.

Evelyn and Natalie are a mother-daughter travel and writing team. They have traveled to seven continents, eighty-eight countries (and counting), and all fifty states.

You can learn more about their travels or reach them to book speaking engagements at their website: www.travelersatheart.com.

TO OUR READERS

Thank you for reading *Have a Love Affair with Travel*. I hope you enjoyed our book and will leave a review on your reading platform choice. Doing so helps other readers find great books.

CONNECT WITH
EVELYN AND NATALIE KELLY
Travelers at Heart

Website:
www.travelersatheart.com

Emails:
travelersatheart@travelersatheart.com

evelyn@travelersatheart.com

natalie@travelersatheart.com

Made in the USA
Columbia, SC
19 September 2025